P9-ELQ-307
God
made
you
to
shine
Étiquettes faciles à peler
Utilisez le gabarit AVERY® 5160®

Gadgets and Gizmos
Published by Orange, a division of The reThink Group, Inc.
5870 Charlotte Lane, Suite 300
Cumming, GA 30040 U.S.A.
The Orange logo is a registered trademark of The reThink Group, Inc.

Other Orange products are available online and direct from the publisher. Visit our website at www.WhatIsOrange.org for more resources like these.

ISBN:978-1-63570-900-1

reThink Conceptual Team: Reggie Joiner, Kristen Ivy, Mike Clear, Dan Scott, Elizabeth Hansen, Elloa Davis
Lead Writer: Brandon O'Dell
Lead Editor: Lauren Terrell
Project Manager: Nate Brandt
Book Design & Additional Illustration: Jacob Hunt

Printed in the United States of America
First Edition 2017

1 2 3 4 5 6 7 8 9 10

04/20/17

Preston,
Thank you for being an amazing kid this week, and I am glad I was able to meet you!
-Yoda (Mikayla)

Uniquely Wired, Wonderfully Made

INTRODUCTION

gadget: (gaj-it)
a mechanical device; any ingenious article

gizmo: (giz-moh)
a gadget

Good day. And welcome to the introduction to this book. This book is called a devotional. If you've never read a devotional before, this introduction will help you know what to expect. If you've never read a book before, don't be alarmed. Simply read the words from left to right and top to bottom until you reach the end of a page. When you've run out of words, gently grasp the top corner of the following page and turn it. Repeat this action until the book is complete.

I'm kidding, of course. I know you've read books before. You're really smart. But since it is possible this is your first devotional, let me explain what a devotional is.

A devotional like this one is for someone who wants to devote or spend their time thinking and learning about God, Jesus, and the Bible. This devotional is called Gadgets and Gizmos because it sounded like a cool name for a devotional. Also because gadgets and gizmos are uniquely created. And you know what else, or rather who else, is uniquely created?

YOU!

You are a one of a kind creation, created by the most creative Creator in the universe! **GOD!**

And with this devotional, you'll learn a little bit more about how creative God is, and about how creative He made you to be. And you'll learn ways you can creatively show and tell others about the love Jesus has for them.

The devotional is split up into nine weeks, five entries per week. You might choose to read the daily entry when you first get up, just after breakfast, before bedtime, or at 3:27 in the afternoon. Whatever you choose, it's probably best to find a routine and stick to it, so you can make reading your devotional into a habit.

At the end of each of the first eight weeks, there's a **TRY THIS** section where you'll be asked to do something a little more than read. Be prepared to go some place, or explore somewhere, or even get a little messy.

Oh! There's one big rule you'll need to follow if you want to get the most out of this devotional:

DO NOT DRAW IN THIS BOOK!

Now take a marker, crayon, pen, or some writing utensil and scribble out the words **"DO NOT"**. Drawing in this book is essential. You'll be asked to answer questions, play games, draw pictures, make up stories, you name it! This book should look like an entirely different book when you're finished with it.

Well, I think that's it. I think you're just about ready to gently grasp the top corner of the next page and turn it. I hope you enjoy discovering how truly unique and creative you are.

BYE!

Drew
PAXton
Danny

WEEK
ONE

DAY 1

God made everything.
(Genesis 1)

This first part is a little dark. A lot dark, actually. Darker than your room at night during a thunderstorm when the power is out and the wind is howling and the thunder is shaking the whole house and your mom and dad aren't home and you're having to take care of your little brother and sister and **EVERYTHING IS GOING HAYWIRE!!!** Sorry. The dark creeps me out.

But that's how dark it was . . . **IN THE BEGINNING!**

Said in a deep Darth Vader-y voice

IN THE BEGINNING, there was nothing. You've heard this story. No stars, no planets, no sun, no earth, no you, no devotional in your hands right now. **NO THING, NOTHING!**

UNTIL . . .

Five letters, Huge word

. . . God said, "Let there be ***light***."

And guess what, when God said, "Let there be light," **THERE WAS LIGHT!**

You can read all about this in your Bible, by the way. The very first page. Well, after you get through the table of contents and all those other pages no one ever reads. I'm talking about the very first page in the book of Genesis.

QUICK TANGENT

You ever wonder what God's voice sounded like? Was there a big, deep echo all over the universe? Or was it more like a whisper? Or does God's voice sound like the wind rustling the tree limbs? I don't know the answer. Just thought I'd ask.

Genesis is a Greek word that means origin or beginning. So, good title for the beginning of the Bible and the origin of the entire universe.

Where was I? Oh, right. God said, "Let there be light," and there was light. And God saw that the light was good. And that was just the first day!

In the days that followed, God not only made light, **He made everything.** Here's the checklist He might have used if God needed checklists:

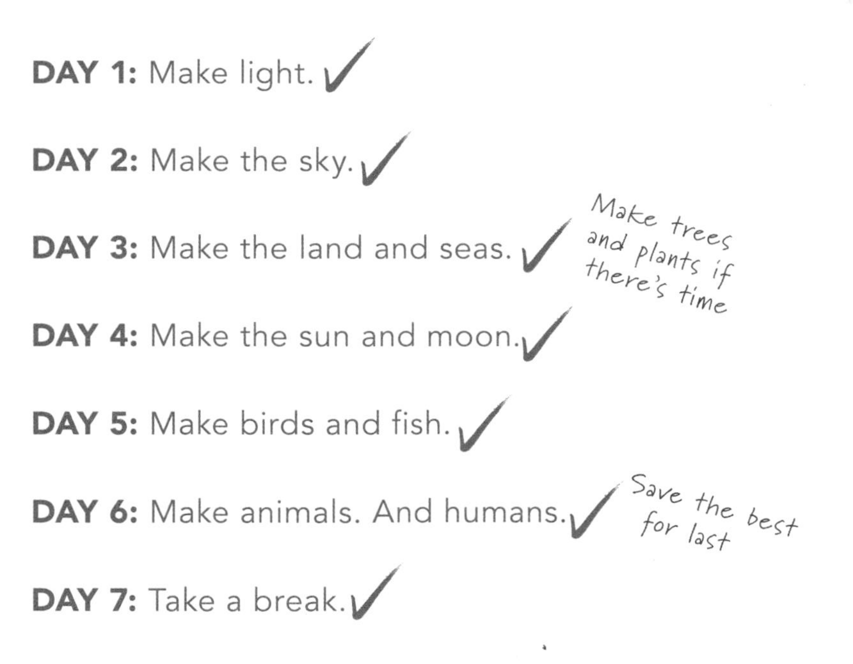

DAY 1: Make light.

DAY 2: Make the sky.

DAY 3: Make the land and seas.

DAY 4: Make the sun and moon.

DAY 5: Make birds and fish.

DAY 6: Make animals. And humans.

DAY 7: Take a break.

Now you might hear some people have discussions about whether or not God made the world in six actual days or if it was six really long periods of time that He called "days." But either way, I think we can all agree that creating the universe and everything in it out of nothing is a pretty amazing accomplishment.

Think about that for a second. **God made everything.**
There was nothing.
Then God spoke.
And there was everything.

And why does that really matter? Because it reminds us just how big, just how powerful, and just how CREATIVE God really is. There is nothing He can't do. Nothing He can't know. No problem He can't solve. **God made everything.** It's so mind blowing, we are going to spend the rest of this week learning about what our big, creative God has made.

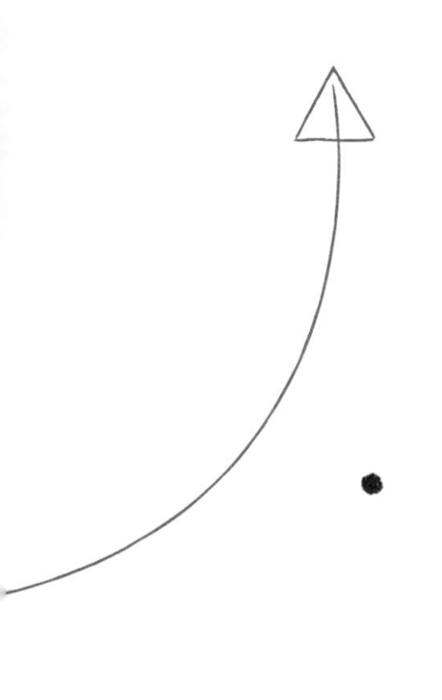

DAY 2

God made the earth.
(Psalm 102:25)

Okay, so we know that God made everything. Everything is a lot of things. It's **EVERY THING!** So let's narrow it down to just a few things God made. Here's a word search coming at you! See how many things you can find in this word search. (**HINT:** they are all things God made.) If you need help, you can find a list of words at the end of today's section.

T V N R L

E A I R B M W Z A

K A L G A E O N B L U

O R A I E I P U P P I E S

M F I S H R N V N J U T N A V

S V X V I N S E C T S Y H U N X A

Y H X E A R T H O A M O O N D B S

Q L O E R R C K U W I N D K I S T H O

J G R A S S L B M S N F R I V E N R F

C W S G Z M D O A E S A N T E L O P E

B P E L I C R T N C E C D T R I C E G

N O S E S L V T S P G E Q E S G E N Q

H N S O E N E R G Y S R N E H A F

T F I N G E R P R I N T S M T N J

R N L S M S K H O V K N E E S

E M K D O L P H I N S I T

E Y A K S J P E F U A

S Y S T A R S G B

A R Q C D

So, yeah, God made lots of things. Let's narrow it down a bit more to just one thing. One BIG thing. The planet Earth. **God made the earth.**

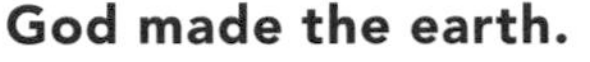

QUICK TANGENT

How many cans of Play-doh would you need to actually make the planet earth? I'm guessing about two million billion cans. I should google that.

Genesis 1:2

The Bible says that in the beginning, the earth was empty and didn't have any shape. That makes me think the earth was like a gigantic ballful of Play-doh floating around in space until God got a hold of it.

Then God shaped the Play-doh into the big, colorful planet we know today, full of mountains and rivers and oceans and trees and hibiscus plants. But, of course, the earth isn't actually made of Play-doh. Science has proven that. You can't deny, however, that the earth is big. It would take over forty thousand football fields connected end to end to make it all the way around the earth. And that would be a really **LOOOOONG** game of football. No one would ever score.

So what does it matter how big the earth is? And so what if it's so beautiful? How does that help you?

Well, it doesn't, unless you keep reminding yourself of one very important thing. **God made the earth.** The earth is big, you say? **God made the earth**, so God must be bigger. The earth is beautiful? **God made the earth**, so God must understand and appreciate beauty. The earth is really heavy, and yet it seems to float in outer space? **God made the earth**, so God must be awfully smart and awfully powerful to make that happen.

When you go outside next time, take a look around you. Look at how beautiful our world is. Look at how big it is. Think of how marvelous it is to be just one planet in our humongous solar system and somehow we don't crash into one another. Then remind yourself, God made all this.

PSALM 102:25 says this —

In the beginning you made the earth secure.
You placed it on its foundations. Your hands created the heavens.

God is big. God is powerful. God knows everything and can do anything. And He loves us enough to create a world full of beauty for us to live in, instead of a lumpy brown ball of Play-doh.

WRITE DOWN SOME THINGS THAT YOU LOVE ABOUT THE EARTH.

....

....

....

....

WHEN YOU SAY YOUR PRAYERS, THANK GOD SPECIFICALLY FOR THE THINGS YOU WROTE DOWN. IN FACT, MAKE A HABIT OF THANKING GOD FOR THE THINGS YOU LOVE ABOUT HIS CREATION. IT WILL HELP YOU NOT TO FORGET HOW BIG AND POWERFUL AND CREATIVE HE IS.

WORD LIST

Earth	puppies
universe	kittens
sky	eagles
stars	dolphins
moon	fingerprints
light	faces
energy	noses
wind	knees
humans	insects
horses	mountains
tigers	rivers
fish	oceans
antelope	grass
trees	bats

DAY 3

God made time.
(Ecclesiastes 3:1)

Design your own planet. Creativity is the key here, so use colored pencils, crayons, stickers, or whatever. Or if you don't like to draw, write a poem or a short story about your planet. Or take a picture of your grandpa's bald head and glue it here. This is about you being creative, not me.

BUT WAIT!!! Before you start, set a timer on your watch or phone or whatever. Keep track of how long it takes you to make your planet. On your mark, get set, go!!!

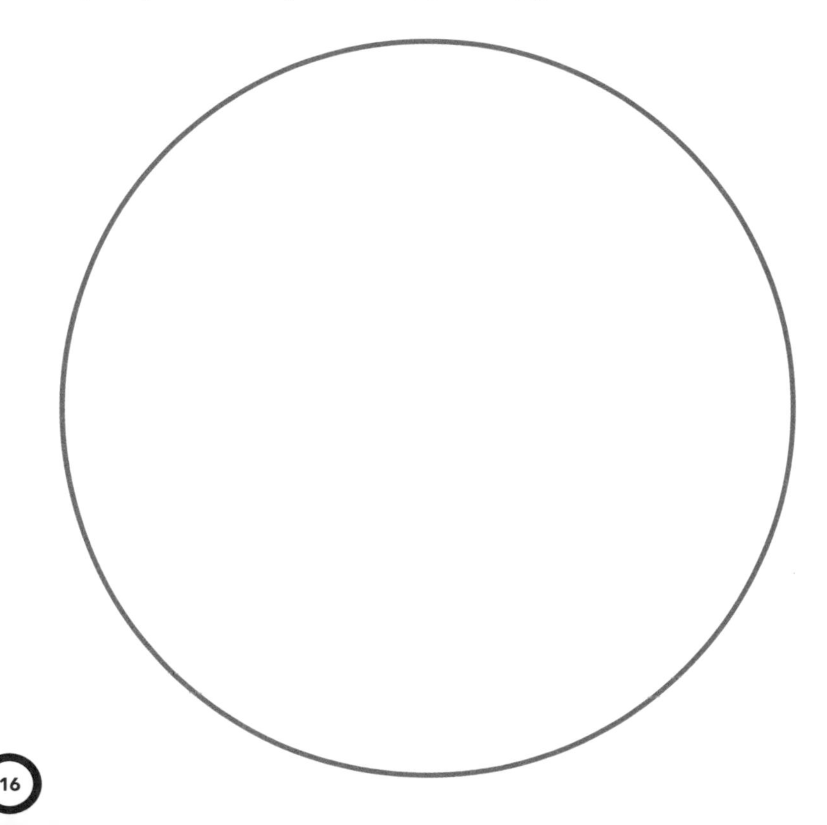

Are you done? Does your planet have a name? ← Might I suggest Baldonia if you went the bald head route.

....

How long did it take you? ....

I hope you didn't feel too rushed. Sometimes when I know I'm being timed, it stresses me out a little. I've gotta hurry. Gotta be the fastest. Gotta win, **WIN, WIN!!!!** Sorry. That's just how I feel sometimes.

Time is very important to a lot of people. Here is what some people have said about time.

"Lost time is never found again."
Benjamin Franklin

"The only reason for time is so that everything doesn't happen at once."
Albert Einstein

"If I could save time in a bottle
The first thing that I'd like to do
Is to save every day 'til eternity passes away
Just to spend them with you."
Jim Croce, "Time in a Bottle"

And one of the wisest men who ever lived wrote this about time in Ecclesiastes 3:1 —

"There is a time for everything.

There's a time for everything that is done on earth."

—King Solomon

King Solomon goes on to write about all the things there are times for. There are times to laugh and cry, a time to dance, a time to speak and a time to be silent, a time to keep and a time to throw away, and many others.

WHAT ARE SOME THINGS YOU MAKE TIME FOR? MAKE A LIST. I'LL START YOU OUT.

Reading your devotional.

Do you ever wonder why you have time to do all those things? Here's something that will blow your mind. **God made time.** He invented it. He made the sun and moon to separate day from night. He made the different seasons. He made time.

Here's why that matters. God is in charge of the whole universe, so He probably doesn't have *time* to worry about people like you and me, right? Wrong! **God made time.** He rules over it and He can use time to do whatever He wants whenever He wants. That means God has time to make it rain in Iowa and make the ocean waves in Mexico. He has time to heal someone who is sick in India and hear a church sing to Him in Japan. God has time to keep the earth moving around the sun, and He has time to listen to your prayers. **God made time!**

TAKE A DEEP BREATH BEFORE YOU PRAY TONIGHT. DON'T RUSH THROUGH YOUR PRAYER. TAKE YOUR TIME. ASK GOD TO HELP YOU KNOW WHAT TO DO WITH THE TIME HE'S GIVEN YOU.

DAY 4

God made the universe.
(Psalm 33:6-7)

Use the clocks below to fill in the times.

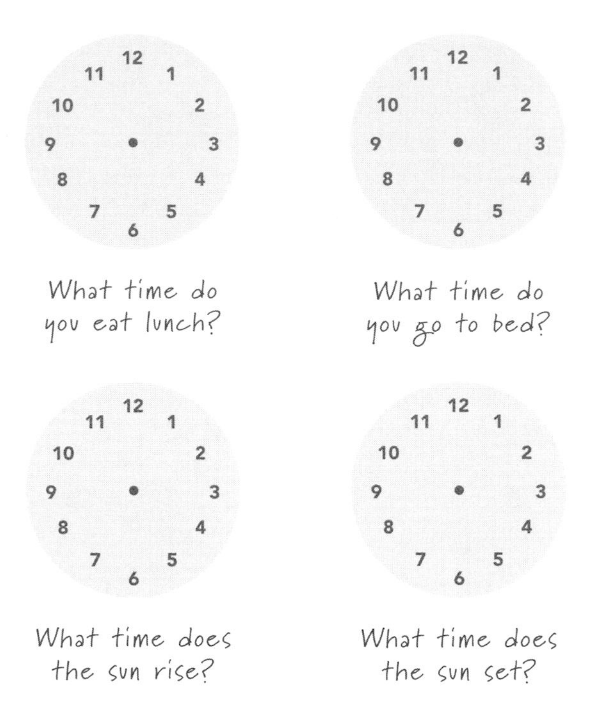

We learned that God made time. He makes the sun rise and the sun set. In fact, God made every single star in the universe. Count the fingers on your hands. Now multiply that number by a 100 million trillion and that's about how many stars there are.

I don't know about you, but I think the universe is amazing. It's so **HUGE!** I mean, think about it. The closest star to the planet earth is the sun, and it's over 90 million miles away!

And get this, a lot of those other tiny little stars you see in the sky are actually bigger than the sun. They're just so far away, they look small. Polaris, or the North Star, is 46 times bigger than the sun and it's over 400 light years away! (I could put that in miles, but I'd get tired writing all the zeros.) Astronomers say there are stars that are 2,000 times bigger than the sun. And probably some **BIGGER!**

Do you feel small yet? I sure do. How did God make all those humongous stars?

Well, Psalm 33:6-7 says —

The heavens were made when the Lord commanded it to happen. All the stars were created by the breath of his mouth. He gathers together the waters of the sea. He puts the oceans in their places.

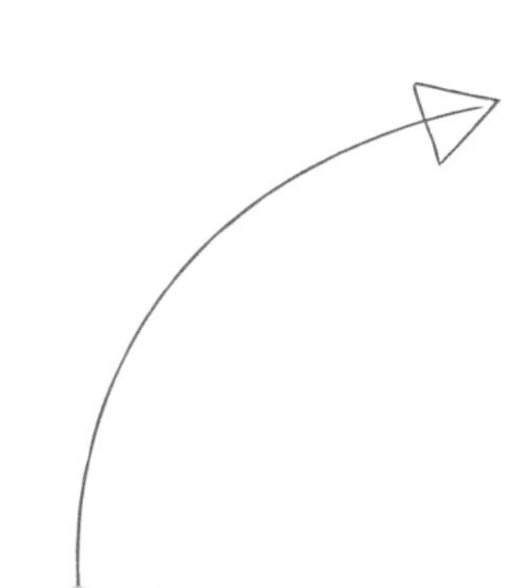

So it was that simple. God just said the words and **He made the universe.** Do you know what I can create just by saying it? Noise. But God's words hold power that we can't even imagine. His very breath can create stars that are 2,000 times bigger than the sun!

IF YOU COULD CREATE SOMETHING WITH JUST YOUR WORDS, WHAT WOULD YOU CREATE?

....

....

....

....

Now see if you can create what you wrote down just by saying it. **HINT:** No, you can't.

There are things in this world only God can do. And that's a great reason to put your faith and trust in Him. **God made the universe.** So He can certainly handle the little problems we encounter day by day. Even our BIG problems are little problems to the Creator of the universe.

DO YOU HAVE ANY PROBLEMS YOU COULD USE GOD'S HELP WITH? WHAT ARE THEY?

....

....

....

....

....

....

....

....

ASK GOD TO HELP YOU WITH THE PROBLEM OR PROBLEMS YOU WROTE DOWN. TRUST THAT HE'S GOT THINGS UNDER CONTROL EVEN IF HE DOESN'T ANSWER YOUR PRAYERS THE WAY YOU EXPECT.

DAY 5

God made the animals.
(Mathew 6:26)

A long time ago, before we had television and YouTube to stare at all day until our brains turned into cheese, people used to look up. At the stars. And they'd look at them so much, they'd start to see shapes called constellations. For instance, there's one called Ursa Major that looks like a big bear.

Sort of . . .

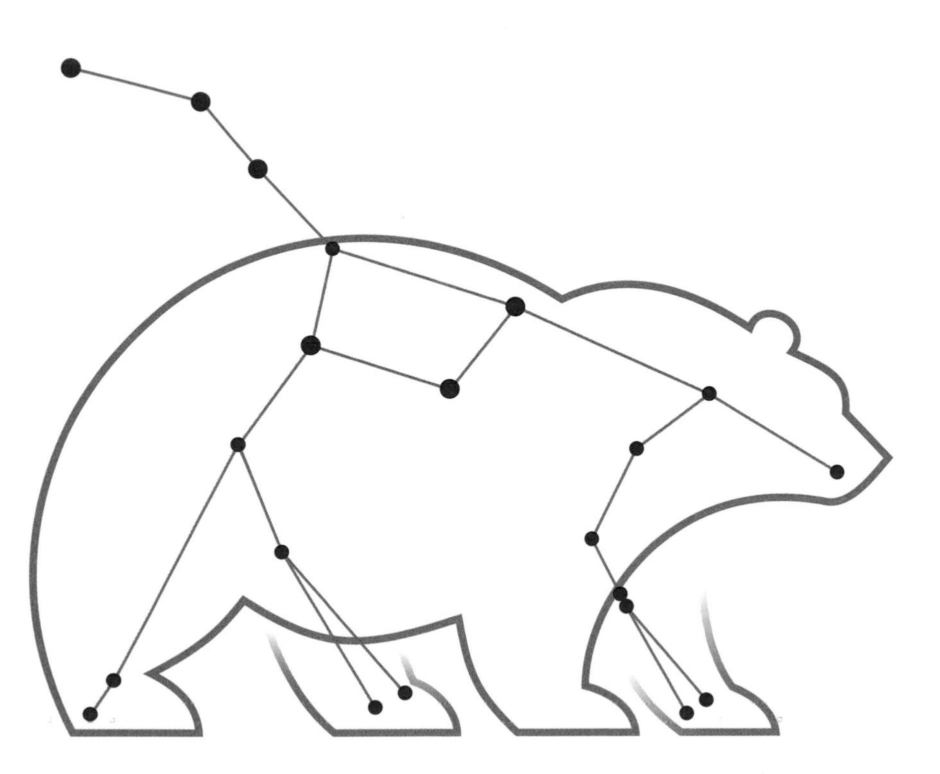

What animal do you see when you look at the constellation below? Connect the stars to make an animal. There's no right answer here. Just use your creativity to see what you can come up with.

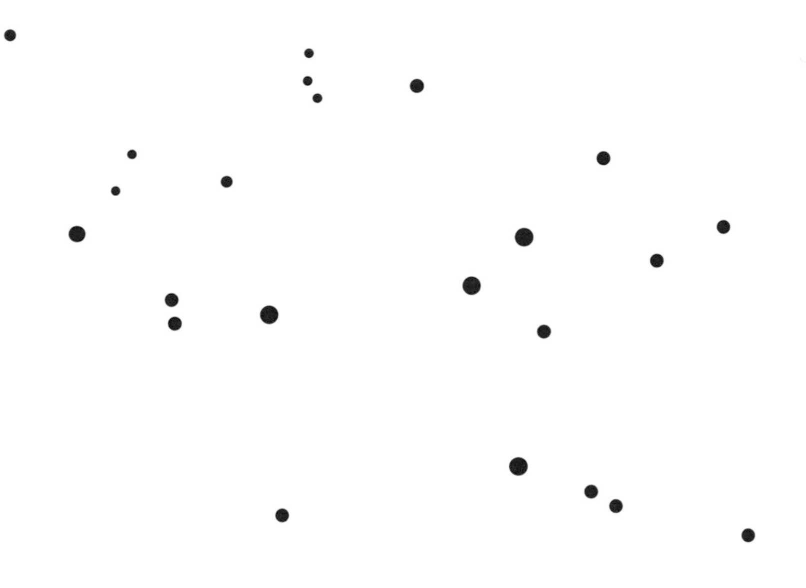

What animal did you see?

....

Show your picture to someone in your family and see what animal they see. Did they see the same animal as you?

I'll bet if you showed your constellation to a thousand people, you'd get a whole bunch of different answers. Mostly because there are **SO** many animals in this world to choose from. One person might see a bear. Another might see a crocodile. Still another might see an endangered South African Gabgoo Bird. And I just made that one up!

The point is there are a lot of animals in the world, of all shapes, sizes and colors. And we learned from the book of Genesis that **God made the animals.** He made the birds in the air, the fish in the sea, and all the creatures that live on the land. God must really love animals.

God's creativity is on full display when you look at the beautiful tail of the peacock, the impossibly tall neck of the giraffe, the nimble feet of the kangaroo, and, of course, the colorful plumage of the Gabgoo Bird.

What is your favorite animal?

....

WHY?

....

....

....

....

God has a favorite creation, too. Something He loves even more than He loves the animals.

YOU.

Read what Jesus said in Matthew 6:26 —

> "Look at the birds of the air. They don't plant or gather crops. They don't put away crops in storerooms. But your Father who is in heaven feeds them. Aren't you worth much more than they are?"

Sure, God loves the birds in the air. And the fish in the sea. And He takes care of all the creatures that live on the land. But the creations that are worth more to Him are people like you and me. There is something about us that's special, and you'll learn exactly what that is next week. If you keep reading, that is.

TRY THIS

Make something.

God made everything out of nothing. But when we make something, we have to have ingredients. Here's what you'll need to make a model of the planet Earth.

- **Yarn**
- **Scissors**
- **Balloon**
- **A bottle of School Glue**
- **½ cup of Corn Starch**
- **¼ cup of Water**

You'll want to ask a grown-up before you start, because creating entire planets can get messy. I suggest making your planet somewhere outside. Only do it inside if you don't mind a bit of clean up afterwards.

unless you're God

Step 1 Blow up the balloon and tie the end. When you blow up the balloon, try to make it as round as possible. This could mean that you don't blow it up all the way.

Step 2 Mix the water, cornstarch, and entire bottle of glue in a mixing bowl. If it's a runny white slime, you mixed it right.

Step 3 Dip the yarn into your gluey mixture and wrap the yarn around the balloon. Keep doing this until you run out of yarn or until you are happy with the way your planet looks. It could look something like this.

Step 4 Let your balloon dry overnight.

Step 5 My favorite part! Pop the balloon!

If everything worked the way it was supposed to, you should now have a big planet shaped ball of yarn. Like this.

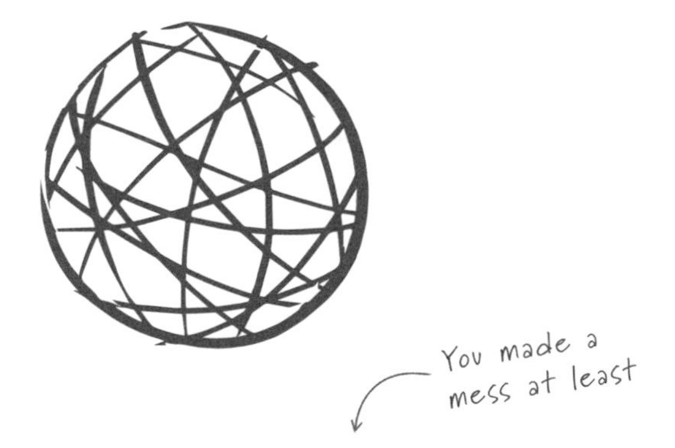

There you have it! You made something! Hopefully this helped you understand how amazing our HUGE creative God is. I wonder how many bottles of glue it took Him to make the real Earth.

WEEK
TWO

DAY 6

God made you. (Genesis 1:27)

Last week, we talked about what God created in the very beginning. The earth, animals, time, the universe!! And the thing God waited until the very end to make: Humans!

> So God created human beings in his own likeness. He created them to be like himself. He created them as male and female.
>
> Genesis 1:27

Here's how it went down in Genesis chapter 2. God made the first man out of the dust in the ground. He breathed the breath of life into him and man came alive. The first man was named Adam. Not long after, God decided to make a helper for Adam, so He caused Adam to fall asleep. God took one of Adam's ribs and from that rib, God made the first woman, whose name was Eve.

QUICK TANGENT

God can do anything! If He can make a man out of dust and a woman out of a rib, I wonder what else He can do. Maybe He can make me a new Porsche out of a potato. Or I've been wanting a puppy. God can probably make one out of my shoe.

So Adam and Eve were the first man and the first woman. And God created a beautiful garden for them to live in called Eden. It was a paradise.

Here's something that I don't want you to miss. God created everything, as you know, but when he created humans, He did something a little bit different. Read Genesis 1:27 one more time. I'll wait.

It says 'God created human beings **in his own likeness**.' Other versions of the Bible say, '...in his own image.' So what does that mean? He didn't create horses in his own likeness. Or dolphins. Or Gabgoo birds! God created humans in His own likeness. Maybe it means that when God looks in a mirror, He sees someone that looks like you. Or maybe it means when humans were created, God gave them certain characteristics that He shared with them.

That would have to be a really big mirror.

So if God is creative, which we know is true, maybe He made humans to be creative. Or if God is loving, maybe humans are made to love. Think about that. Here are just a few words that describe what God can be like. Circle the ones that sound like you.

Creative	**Loving**	**Generous**	**Smart**
Patient	**Kind**	**Joyful**	**Gentle**
Good	**Just**	**Forgiving**	**Strong**

No other creature on the planet was created in God's image. Just humans. Which, by the way, you are one. **God made you.** And this week, we're going to learn a little bit about how you should treat the you that God made.

DAY 7

Take care of your body.
(1 Corinthians 6:19-20)

Okay, self-portrait time. It's time for you to create you. But instead of just drawing a picture, try finding pictures of facial features that look like you in magazines or on the internet, cut them out and piece them together to make a kind of a jigsaw puzzle of your face. Use the space below (or a separate piece of paper if you need more room) to create your face.

Ask your parents before you start cutting up their magazines.

God made you. The creator of the entire universe made you. So now you have a responsibility.

Think of it this way. Someone just gave you a brand new cell phone. But not just any cell phone. This is the latest model, the only one like it in the whole world. It's got the best camera you've ever seen. A million different games. You can text or talk with your friends from inside a cave if you wanted. And it can predict the future. How are you going to treat your new phone? Are you going to play catch with it? Would you leave it out in the street? Would you drop it in your toilet? Of course not. You're going to take care of it. You're going to protect it from harm and use it the way it was meant to be used.

So God made you. You are the only one like you in the whole world. How are you going to treat yourself? Are you going to run into the street without looking? Are you going to eat a bunch of junk food and never brush your teeth? Will you watch TV all day long and never get any exercise? You're probably going to say, "no" to all of those questions, because you know that's what you're supposed to say. But the truth is, everybody has the tendency to mistreat the body God has given them.

But we really shouldn't do that. And here's a big reason why.

Don't you know that your bodies are temples of the Holy Spirit? The Spirit is in you, and you have received the Spirit from God. You do not belong to yourselves. Christ has paid the price for you. So use your bodies in a way that honors God.

1 Corinthians 6:19-20

Your body is a temple? What in the world does that mean? Well, it helps to know a little bit of history. The book of Exodus tells the story of Moses and the Israelites escaping from slavery in Egypt. And it tells about how they wandered in the desert for forty years. While they wandered, they took a huge tent with them, called the tabernacle. It was the place where they could worship God and offer sacrifices. And it was the place God sent His Spirit to live. Many years later, King Solomon built a temple that took the place of the tabernacle, a permanent home for the Holy Spirit of God.

But then...when God sent Jesus to die for our sins, the Holy Spirit went to live in the hearts of all who believed in Jesus. So the body became the temple.

And that's why you should **take care of your body.**

WHAT ARE SOME THINGS YOU DO TO TAKE CARE OF YOUR BODY?

....

....

....

....

....

....

....

....

WHAT ARE SOME THINGS YOU COULD DO BETTER?

....

....

....

....

....

....

....

....

....

If you wrote something down that you could do better, try doing just one of those things this week. It could be eating just one more vegetable than usual. It could be flossing your teeth. It could be playing outside instead of playing video games. Just keep reminding yourself to **take care of your body** because it is God's temple.

Honor your family.
(Exodus 20:12)

Since your body was made by the creator of the universe, the least you can do is take care of it. So, do what your mom says and eat all your fruits and vegetables. Draw a line from the healthy food to the giant mouth.

Why, oh why, can't ice cream be a vegetable? Then it would be easier to do what Mom wanted. Moms and Dads are always telling you to do things that are "good for you." Which we know means "not fun and unpleasant."

Brush your teeth.
Floss your teeth.
Gargle mouthwash.

Don't swim after eating.
Look both ways before crossing the street.

WHAT ARE SOME THAT I MISSED?

....

....

....

....

And you have to do what they want or you'll get in trouble. So roll your eyes, stomp around and obey your parents. Or maybe there's another way.

Honor your father and mother.

Exodus 20:12

What does it mean to honor someone? It means when they enter the room, you should applaud.

"WOO-HOO! Yay, Dad! You're the best!"

Or maybe it means you should buy them a trophy.

"And the award for best Grandma in the country goes to...MEEMAW!"

Truth is, there are a lot of different ways we can honor someone. It's simply finding ways to show someone how valuable they are. Trophies and applause would work, but there are simpler ways as well. You could do what they ask without stomping or rolling your eyes. You could say, 'please' when you want something, and 'thank you' when your folks do something nice for you. You could help out when you see someone is doing a job all alone.

WHAT ARE SOME OTHER WAYS YOU CAN SHOW SOMEONE THEY'RE IMPORTANT OR VALUABLE?

....

....

....

....

Exodus 20:12 says to honor your father and mother, but I think we should take that a step further. There are a lot of boys and girls who don't have a mom and dad. Some kids live with their grandparents, some with stepparents, some with foster parents, some with aunts and uncles, some with aliens. So more than just mother and father, you should **honor your family.**

I made up the alien part... I think.

WRITE DOWN WHO'S IN YOUR IMMEDIATE FAMILY. WHO LIVES WITH YOU RIGHT NOW AND HOW ARE THEY RELATED TO YOU?

....

....

....

....

....

....

....

....

Just like you take care of your body because God made it, it's important to treat your family with honor and respect because God has given you your family. And it's the only one you've got.

Here's a challenge for you. Sometime before the next devotional entry, try to find a way to honor somebody in your family. It doesn't have to be a huge thing. Just remember what it is, because I'm going to ask you about it later.

DAY 9

Be a good friend.
(Proverbs 17:17)

We've learned that God made you and since you are in charge of you, you have a responsibility to take care of the you God made. One way you can do that is by taking care of your body. Another is by honoring your family. I gave you a challenge after yesterday's entry.

WRITE DOWN HOW YOU CHOSE TO HONOR A FAMILY MEMBER.

....

....

....

....

....

....

....

....

....

....

....

That's great!

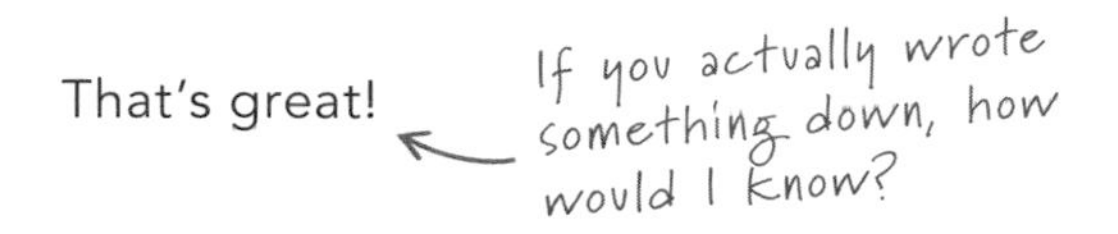

But your responsibilities aren't over yet, I'm afraid. Because there's another important group of people God has placed in your life. They're the people you spend the most time with besides your family. Your friends!

Here's one of the things the Bible says about friendship —

A friend loves at all times. They are there to help when trouble comes.

Proverbs 17:17

POP QUIZ TIME. DO YOUR BEST TO ANSWER THE FOLLOWING MULTIPLE CHOICE QUESTIONS. PLEASE USE A NUMBER 2 PENCIL.

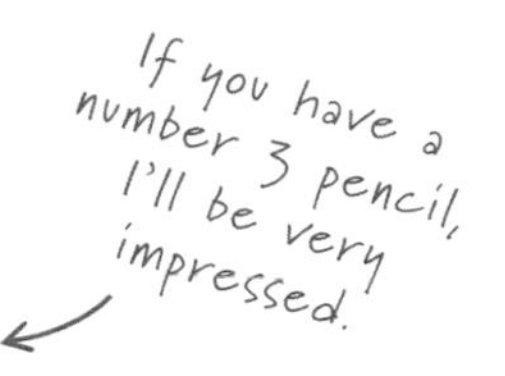

1. **You and your friend are invited to a birthday pool party, but your friend has never learned how to swim. Would a good friend...**
   - **a.** Make fun of the friend in front of everyone?
   - **b.** Push them in the deep end and see what happens?
   - **c.** Spend some time in the shallow end so they don't get lonely?
   - **d.** Drain the pool so nobody can swim?

2. **You're at a pizza party and you and your friend both reach for the last piece of pepperoni. Would a good friend...**
   - **a.** Throw the piece at the friend and scream, 'FINE! YOU TAKE IT!'
   - **b.** Find a way to split the piece in half?
   - **c.** Pretend you don't see them and eat the piece quickly?
   - **d.** Lick the pepperonis?

3. **On a camping trip, you and your friend get lost on a hike. Would a good friend...**
   - **a.** Stick together until you find your way back?
   - **b.** Knock your friend over and shout, 'FREE BEAR FOOD OVER HERE!'
   - **c.** Blame your friend for not paying attention to the guide?
   - **d.** Run away and let your friend fend for themselves?

I hope you got all the right answers. But if you need help, read Proverbs 17:17 one more time. "A friend loves at all times. They are there to help when trouble comes."

You may have lots of friends. You may only have a few. You may still be working on finding a good friend. But whatever the case, God wants you to **be a good friend**, which means loving others, and just being there when they need help.

WRITE DOWN THE NAMES OF SOME OF YOUR FRIENDS.

....

....

....

....

....

....

Ask God to help you look for ways to **be a good friend** to them.

DAY 10

Treat others the way you want to be treated. (Luke 6:31)

God made you, and you're responsible for your body, how you treat your family and friends, and you're responsible for one other very important thing.

Shoes.

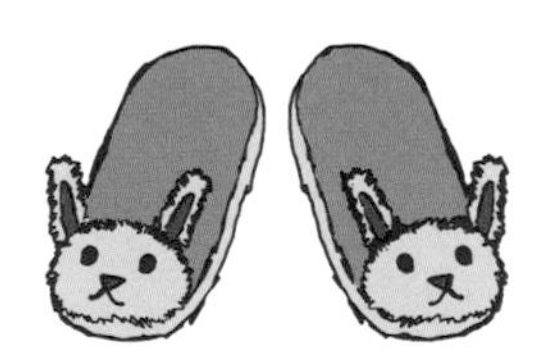

What kind of person would wear these shoes? Which ones would you wear?

Okay, you're not responsible for shoes exactly, but you are responsible for how you treat the people who wear these or any kind of shoes. (And barefoot people, too) In short, everyone you meet.

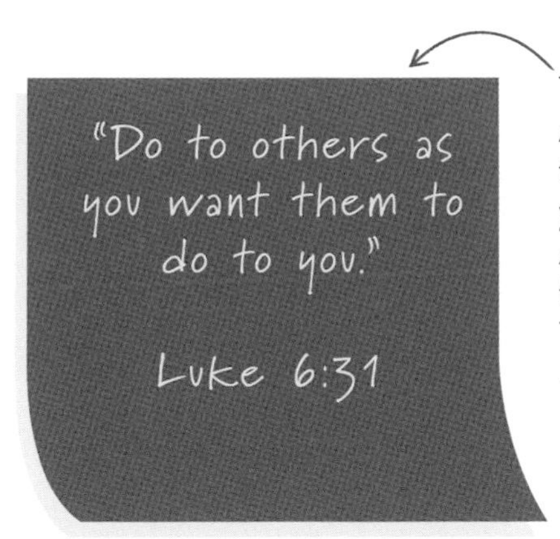

That's what Jesus said. Another way of putting it is this – **Treat others the way you want to be treated.** And that's not just your family and your friends. That's your neighbors, your acquaintances, people who act or believe differently than you, and really anyone you come across.

Sometimes you have to put yourself in another person's shoes, so you'll have a better understanding how they want to be treated. For instance, imagine you're having a picnic. You're out at the park. It's a nice, breezy summer afternoon. You've got your PB&J and tall glass of freshly-squeezed lemonade. Everything is perfect. Until this kid named Steve kicks a soccer ball right into the middle of it all, knocking over your lemonade and smushing your sandwich. Now your first instinct might be to get mad, throw a tantrum, and threaten to keep the soccer ball. Or...you could put yourself in Steve's muddy soccer cleats.

If you were Steve, having fun playing soccer, you might not notice the family having a picnic nearby. You're too busy having a good time. So kicking the soccer ball in their direction could be an honest mistake.

If you thought it through like that, would it change the way you reacted to the runaway soccer ball? Do you think you would respond with more patience and understanding?

Putting yourself in another person's shoes gives you a different perspective. And it works in a lot of different situations.

Someone forgot to bring their lunch to school. Would you want someone to help you if you forgot your lunch?

A new kid at school looks lost. Would you want someone to show you the way if you were new?

A neighbor breaks their leg and has to wear a cast. Would you want someone to check up on you if your leg was broken?

There are a lot of ways to help people if you just keep your eyes open and **treat others the way you want to be treated.** So here's a challenge for you. Be on the lookout for people in need over the next few days. Imagine what it would be like to walk in their shoes. And all next week, you'll be learning how to put your imagination into action.

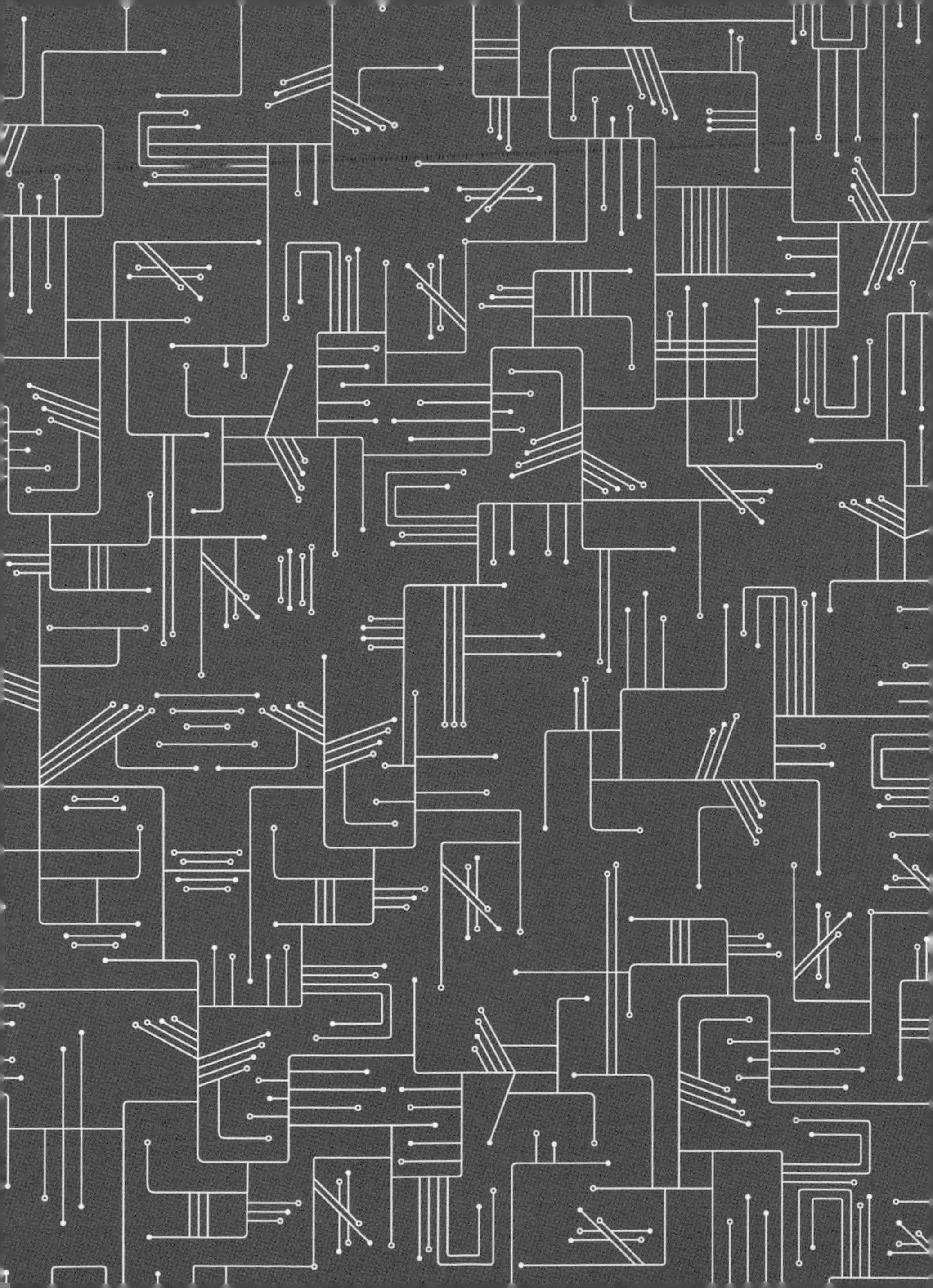

TRY THIS

Take care of something.

When God made you, He gave you a lot to take care of:

- **Your body**
- **Your friends**
- **Your family**
- **Other people**
- **The planet**

So how about some practice taking care of something.

You'll need a grownup's help to get started with this one. If you already have a plant at your home, that can be the thing you take care of. OR you can buy a potted plant at your local gardening store. If you'd rather start from scratch, here's what you'll need:

- **A small flowerpot**
- **Some potting soil**
- **Flower seeds**
- **Water**
- **Sunshine**

Step 1 Find the right flowerpot, the right soil, and the right seeds. You can ask someone who works at your local gardening store to help you get started. Or you can go online and search "What kind of flowers work in flowerpots?"

Step 2 Put the potting soil in your flowerpot.

Step 3 Poke holes for the seeds. Not too deep.

Step 4 Drop your seeds in the holes.

Step 5 Water your seeds. Not too much water. You don't want to drown them out.

Step 6 Make sure the flowerpot is placed in sunlight.

Step 7 Water your seeds every day and wait for them to grow.

A plant takes a lot of care to help it grow. It's the same with you. You need a lot of care to help you grow. And it's the same with your relationships, with God and with others. They all take care to help them grow.

So practice on the plant, then you'll be ready to take care of the more important things.

WEEK
THREE

DAY 11

God made you to imagine.
(Genesis 2:19-20)

Let's review. In the beginning, God made the earth and everything on it, plants, animals, humans. The name of the first man was Adam, and he lived in a beautiful garden called Eden. And there was a lot of work to be done. There were all these birds and animals and none of them had names. So God gave Adam the task of naming them all.

Hint: It wasn't English

> The Lord God had formed all the wild animals and all the birds in the sky. He had made all of them out of the ground. He brought them to the man to see what names He would give them. And the name the man gave each living creature became its name.
> Genesis 2:19

Now we don't know what language Adam spoke. So we don't really know what names he came up with. But we can guess that Adam had to have quite the imagination to come up with so many different animal and bird names.

Adam: Let's see. To that four legged spotted animal with the really tall neck. I will call you...Spotted Tallneckatron! And to the large gray fellow there with the long nose that sounds like a trumpet when you sneeze. You shall now be known as...Jumbo Trumpetasaurus. To the small furry creature with the floppy ears and fluffy tail. I shall call you...Harold.

MAYBE IT WENT SOMETHING LIKE THAT.

We know that humans were created in God's likeness, which would help explain how Adam was able to name all those animals. God clearly has an incredible imagination. And His imagination shows up big time in Adam.

How else could you explain the platypus?

That must mean that God's imagination shows up in you and me, too. It's true! **God made you to imagine.**

Think about that! You're created in God's likeness! And He's given you your imagination! One day, you might design a skyscraper with your imagination. You might write a novel. Or name a star. Or cure a disease. Or invent something that will change the world.

QUICK TANGENT

Here's an invention idea for you — food glue. You know when you're eating a Pop Tart and it breaks apart before you're done eating. It would be great if you could glue it back together with some edible glue. It could come in different colors and flavors. I'd invent it myself, but I'm busy writing this devotional.

You may not be asked to use your imagination to name all the animals in the world, but somehow, you'll make your mark using your imagination, either by helping others, honoring God, or any number of ways. And that's exactly what you will learn to do this week—imagine that!

DAY 12

Use your imagination to make your mark. (Romans 12:6-8)

All right. Let's get that imagination working. **If you were given the assignment to name these animals, what would you call them?**

Use the space provided to come up with your own animal, something that's never existed. You can draw a picture of it or use words to describe it. Don't forget to name this animal, too.

Guess what. If you followed instructions, you just created something that no one's ever seen before. You've used your imagination to make something brand new!

The imagination is an incredible thing. God, we know, is very creative and imaginative. And since we were created in His image, that must mean we're imaginative, too. Everybody has an imagination, and everybody's imagination is different.

Here's a list of things that people use their imaginations for. **CIRCLE THE ONES THAT SOUND LIKE YOU.**

Drawing	**Playing games**	**Designing Buildings**
Science	**Telling jokes**	**Solving problems**
Singing	**Cooking**	**Fixing broken things**
Painting	**Baking**	**Video Games**
Telling stories	**Dancing**	**Gardening**
Writing poems	**Computers**	**Cleaning**
Acting	**Math**	**Music**

Is there something I missed? ....

The Bible talks about other ways we can use our imaginations.

We all have gifts. They differ according to the grace God has given to each of us.

Romans 12:6

And then, Paul, who wrote the book of Romans, goes on to list some of the gifts God has given people.

PROPHECY This isn't like telling the future or anything. It's more like a gift a preacher might have. Someone who is good at telling other people about Jesus and about God's wisdom from the Bible.

SERVING This is someone who loves to serve others. Someone who gets joy out of helping people in need.

TEACHING Someone who is good at teaching people new things, or making complicated things seem simple.

ENCOURAGING That person who's always trying to cheer someone up, someone who's going to tell you, "You can do it!" when things seem impossible.

GIVING This is a gift giver, the person who doesn't need a special occasion to send a card and buy a present. This person is very generous.

LEADING This is the person you go to when you need someone to take charge. They have a plan and they know how to make things happen.

SHOWING MERCY This person forgives people who have let them down. They're the ones you go to when you're looking for a second chance.

Maybe one of those gifts sounds like you. Maybe one of the others sounds like someone you know—someone who has left the impression of being super generous or encouraging. Now it's your turn to make sure you leave an impression, a mark. It's your turn to use your imagination to make your mark. No matter what you're good at, the important thing is to use the gifts you've been given. An unused imagination is pretty worthless. So use it to make your unique mark on the world.

THINK ABOUT THE WAYS YOU CAN USE YOUR IMAGINATION, THE THINGS YOU CIRCLED EARLIER OR THE THINGS PAUL LISTED IN ROMANS. ASK GOD TO SHOW YOU HOW YOU CAN USE YOUR IMAGINATION FOR HIM.

DAY 13

Use your imagination to help others. (1 Peter 4:10)

See if you can unscramble the names of these people whose imaginations helped them make their mark.

BLERAT SEEINNTI made his mark in the area of physics, most notably developing the theory of relativity.

INL-ANLMEU MDARANI won the Pulitzer Prize for his Broadway musical based on the life of Alexander Hamilton.

NAIID ZMLEEN won a Tony award for portraying a Wicked witch and we still can't let go of the song she sang in the movie, Frozen.

ALAMEI RHRATAE was the first woman to fly an airplane solo across the Atlantic Ocean.

KABRCA MOABA was the first African-American President of the United States.

TSMHOA DSEINO contributed to the invention of, among other things, the phonograph, the movie camera, and the incandescent light bulb.

Who knows? Maybe your name will be scrambled in somebody's devotional one day because of your imagination. It's nice to have goals.

As I've mentioned, there are lots of different ways to use your imagination, but Peter, one of Jesus' disciples talks about one very important way —

> God's gifts of grace come in many forms. Each of you has received a gift in order to serve others. You should use it faithfully.
>
> 1 Peter 4:10

Did you catch that middle sentence? Whatever gift you've been given, you have been given it so that you can serve others. Okay, maybe it's not so easy to serve others with your ability to touch your tongue to your nose or write your name holding the pencil with your toes. But that's where your imagination comes in! Get creative—**use your imagination to help others.**

For instance, if your gift is that you're good at basketball, you might serve others by asking your new neighbor to come over and play. Or you could play a charity game to raise money for something you care about. Or you could help your mom do the laundry by pretending the washing machine is a basketball hoop.

WHAT ARE SOME WAYS YOU COULD HELP OTHERS IF YOU HAD THESE GIFTS?

Singing

....

....

Computers

....

....

Teaching

....

....

NOW WRITE DOWN ONE OF YOUR GIFTS.

....

WHAT ARE SOME WAYS YOU CAN USE YOUR GIFT TO SERVE OTHERS?

....

....

....

....

This is where having an imagination really comes in handy. You can find creative ways to help people by doing the things you're good at and that you enjoy doing. Helping others shouldn't have to feel like a burden. If we all used our imaginations to help others, we could make a big difference in the world.

WHEN YOU PRAY TODAY, ASK GOD TO HELP YOU KEEP A LOOKOUT FOR PEOPLE WHO NEED HELP. THEN USE THE GIFTS HE'S GIVEN YOU TO HELP THEM.

DAY 14

Use your imaginations together. (Hebrews 10:24)

You've learned that it's important to use your imagination to help others. Well, for this next exercise, see if you can find someone who can use his or her imagination to help you complete this story I wrote. Without letting them see the story, ask them to help fill in the blanks.

Once there was a boy named Nathan. Nathan was a very .... (adjective) boy. One day, Nathan went to the .... (place), because he loved animals. When he got there, Nathan realized there was trouble. All of the .... (animal (plural)) had gotten out of their cages. People were .... (-ing verb) around in a panic. "What should we do," they .... (-ed verb), "Isn't there someone here who can solve this .... (noun)?" "I've got a(n) .... (noun)," said Nathan. He was very .... (adjective) after all. "I'll play my .... (instrument) to make the .... (plural animal) fall asleep. Then we can .... (verb) them back to their cages." Without delay, Nathan .... (-ly adverb) played his .... (instrument). And all through the .... (place), people could hear the .... (-ing verb) of the .... (animal (plural)), as they .... (-ly adverb) drifted off to sleep. Nathan was a hero! The people picked him up and carried Nathan on their .... (body part (plural))! Nathan's imagination had truly saved the .... (noun).

Make sure you read the story out loud when you're finished.

Sometimes imaginations work better when you work together. Hebrews 10:24 says —

> Let us consider how we can stir up one another to love. Let us help one another to do good works.

If you were to paint your bedroom by yourself, it would probably take a really long time. But if you got somebody to help you, you could get it done faster.

The same is true when we use our imaginations. You can get a lot done when you use your imagination, but you can accomplish even more when you **use your imaginations together.** And it's even better when you use your imagination with someone whose imagination is different from yours.

For instance, let's say you're really good at math. What if you worked together with someone who's really good at telling stories? The two of you could write a story about math that helps simplify math for people who aren't so good at it.

Or if you're a good singer, maybe you could work together with someone who's good at telling jokes. You could write funny songs that help cheer people up.

Choose two of the talented people below and come up with a way the two of them could work together. There's no right answer here. Just use your imagination.

Soccer Coach
Artist
Ballerina
Rock Star
Eye Doctor
Teacher
Fire Fighter
Preacher
Veterinarian
Mail Carrier

Read Hebrews 10:24 one more time. "Let us consider how we can stir up one another to love. Let us help one another to do good works." Let that be your prayer tonight. Ask God to help you consider how you can **use your imaginations** together to love others and do good works.

DAY 15

Use your imagination to honor God. (Colossians 3:23a)

You know now that God made you to imagine. And you can use your imagination in a number of ways. You can use it to love and help others, to do good works, and you can use your imagination to make your mark in the world. And if you work together with others, you can accomplish more than you can do alone. Today you'll learn about another way you can use your imagination, maybe the most important way—**to honor God.**

I don't know what you think of when you think of honoring God. Maybe something like this:

Now I'm not saying that's a bad thing. God could use a cheerleader every once in awhile. And He's certainly deserving of it. In fact, what are some reasons God deserves to be honored?

....

....

....

Here are a few more if you didn't get these already.
Some reasons we should honor God are:

1. God made everything.
2. God made the earth.
3. God made the universe
4. God made **YOU!**

There are many more reasons, of course, but that will get us started.

Which brings us back to how.
How do you honor God?

Colossians 3:23a has one answer —

Work at everything you do with all your heart. Work as if you were working for the Lord...

That means *whatever* you do, work at it with all your heart. You don't have to be a preacher to honor God. You don't have to be a missionary in the jungles of Africa to honor God. You can honor God simply by doing your best at whatever you choose to do.

Match the occupation with the way they can honor God.

Teacher	**Cheer their best**
Actor	**Teach their best**
Cheerleader	**Lead the country their best**
Postal Carrier	**Sell their best**
President	**Deliver mail their best**
Salesman	**Act their best**

If you choose to play soccer, play your best. If you're cleaning your room, clean your best. If you're playing a tree in the school musical, be the best tree you can be. And don't do it so everyone will see how great you are, but so that everyone will see how great God is. "Work as if you were working for the Lord..." **Use your imagination to honor God.**

GOD DESERVES TO BE HONORED. WE'VE SEEN JUST A FEW OF THE REASONS. AND NEXT WEEK, YOU'LL LEARN ABOUT THE BIGGEST REASON OF ALL.

TRY THIS

Imagine something.

Earlier this week, you were given the task of creating a new kind of animal on paper, either by drawing it or describing it. What was the name of your animal?

....

Your imagination will be a very useful tool in your life. You'll be able to use your imagination to create new things, to come up with new ideas, and to solve problems. And you've got to give your imagination a work out from time to time, so let's bring your animal to life. Okay, not really ALIVE alive, but at least it'll be three-dimensional.

Go back and look at the animal you came up with and think of the best way to make a 3-D version of it. You can use clay or Play-Doh, Wikki stix, construction paper, cardboard and duct tape. Nothing is off the table. Or you could use my favorite art supply – trash.

Go online and search "animals made from trash" and you'll see some amazing sculptures using common household items. This one's my favorite.

I can't really give you specific instructions on how to build your animal, because I don't know what it looks like. Use your imagination and make your animal as close to its picture or description.

When you're done, take a picture of your 3-D animal and tape it here.

That way you can always remember what you made.

God has a **HUGE** imagination! And since God made you in His image, you have a **HUGE** imagination, too! So give it a work out. Don't let a good imagination go to waste.

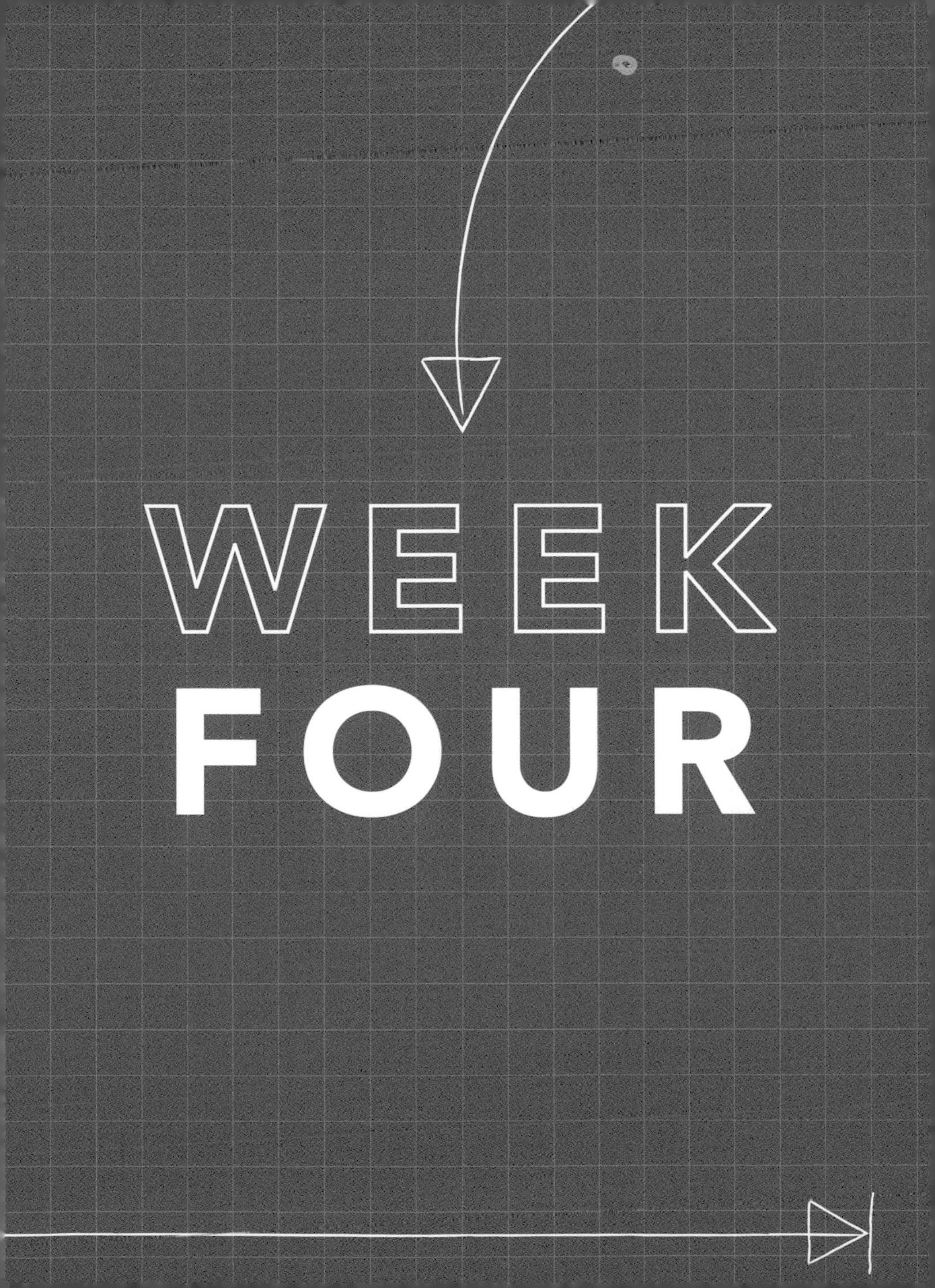
WEEK
FOUR

DAY 16

God made you to know him. (Genesis 3)

Let's start at the beginning one more time. In the beginning, God made the heavens and the earth. He made the stars and the planets. He made the animals. He made the first man and woman, Adam and Eve. And He gave them a beautiful paradise to live in, the Garden of Eden. Adam and Eve were made to live in paradise in a close relationship with God. Everything was pretty much perfect.

And then there was . . . **THE TREE.**

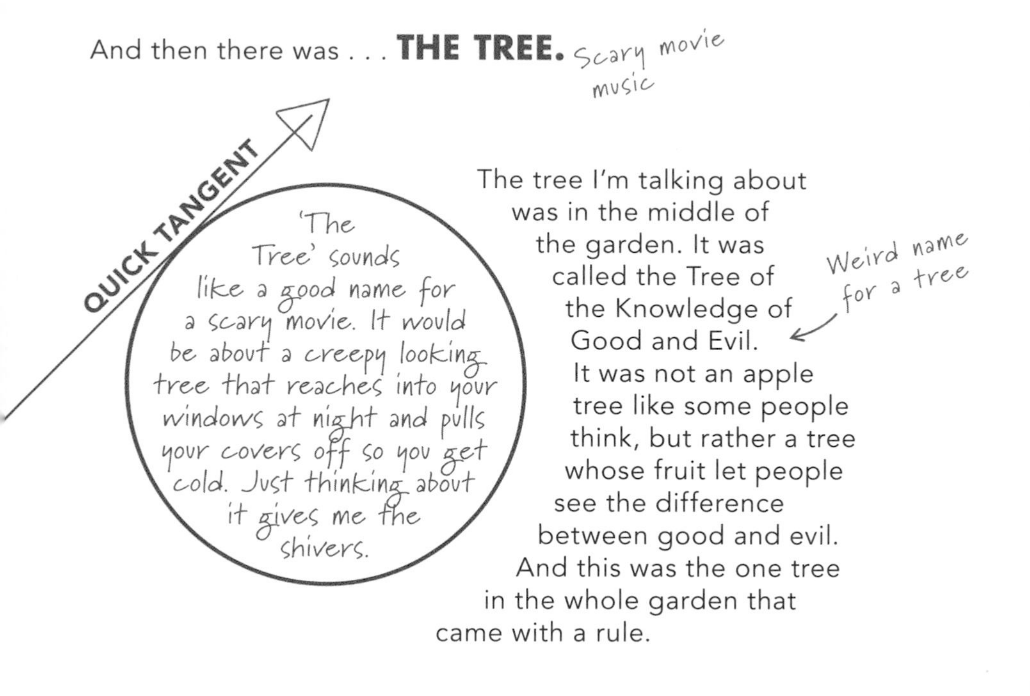

The tree I'm talking about was in the middle of the garden. It was called the Tree of the Knowledge of Good and Evil. It was not an apple tree like some people think, but rather a tree whose fruit let people see the difference between good and evil. And this was the one tree in the whole garden that came with a rule.

God said, "You may eat fruit from any tree in the garden. But you must not eat the fruit from the tree of the knowledge of good and evil. If you do, you will certainly die."

So this tree was bad news.
Don't mess with . . . **THE TREE.** Scary movie music

You probably know what happened next. If not, you can read Genesis chapter 3.

Here's a play by play.

1. A talking serpent convinces Eve to eat the forbidden fruit.
2. Eve convinces Adam to take a bite.
3. God finds out.
4. Adam and Eve (and the serpent) get punished.

The punishment is very severe. God put a curse on the ground so it took a lot of hard work to get food to grow. He made it painful for Eve to have children. He banished Adam and Eve from paradise. And He made it so they could die.

In Genesis 3:19, God says —

"You were made out of the ground. You will return to it when you die. You are dust, and you will return to dust."

Adam and Eve's close relationship with God was over. Paradise was gone. They broke God's rule and sin entered into the world.

This story is tragic. Because God made Adam and Eve to know Him. But they blew it. And do you know what? **God made you to know Him**, too. But sin is still in the world. It has been passed down from generation to generation. So you and I can't live in paradise. And you can't have the close relationship with God that you were made for. **UNLESS...** God makes a way. And you'll find out this week that God had a plan all along to do just that.

DAY 17

God made a promise.
(Isaiah 9:6)

If you got to live in paradise, what would it look like? Sunshine and palm trees? A mansion with an indoor basketball court? A world full of waterslides?

Draw a picture or describe with words what your paradise would look like in the space below.

Adam and Eve were made to live in paradise, the garden of Eden. But they broke God's rule, so they were punished.

Take your pencil and scribble over what you drew or wrote above.

When Adam and Eve ate from **THE TREE**, everything was ruined. They were kicked out of paradise. And not only that, they were separated from God. And ever since, sin has kept people from a close relationship with God, and there is no hope for anybody.

And that's the end of the devotional.

BUT WAIT! Don't stop reading just yet! Maybe there is hope after all, because **God made a promise.**

Have you ever made a promise? What was it?

....

....

Have you ever broken a promise? (Circle one)

YES NO

Well, when God makes a promise, He keeps it. Every time. All the time. Forever and ever. And God's promise came through a prophet named Isaiah. God spoke to Isaiah and Isaiah wrote it all down in a book that's in the Bible.

That's pronounced eye-ZAY-uh.

A few thousand years after Adam and Eve, Isaiah wrote, "The people who are now living in darkness will see a great light."

That sounds like hope to me! People were in a really dark place after they got kicked out of paradise BUT Isaiah says there's light at the end of the tunnel.

Then Isaiah wrote —

A child will be born to us.
A son will be given to us.
He will rule over us. And
He will be called Wonderful
Adviser and Mighty God.
He will also be called Father
Who Lives Forever and
Prince Who Brings Peace.

Isaiah 9:6

Sounds like this child would be pretty special. **God made a promise** to send this child to save us from the sin that separated us from Him. The child would be our light. He would be our hope. He would bring us peace. He would be our Savior. I know who the child is. Do you?

THINK OF GOD'S PROMISE TONIGHT AND THINK ABOUT WHAT IT MEANS TO YOU. ARE YOU GRATEFUL THAT HE KEEPS HIS PROMISES? TELL HIM SO.

DAY 18

God sent His Son. (Luke 2:10-11)

God made you to know Him, but sin makes that really hard for you since sin keeps people separated from God. Fortunately, God loves you so much He promised to make a way to bring you back to Him. A child would be born who would bring a peace that would never end.

And that child's name was ....

Hopefully you wrote **JESUS**, because that's the answer I was looking for.

There was a time, two thousand or so years ago, when people didn't know the answer to that question. They knew God had promised a child who would grow up to be their Savior. They called him the Messiah, a Hebrew word meaning "chosen one." But they didn't know when He would be born or what His name would be.

People waited for hundreds of years after Isaiah wrote about the promised Savior. Some people started to lose hope. Many forgot about the promise altogether. But God is patient and He waited for the perfect time and place for the baby to be born.

The place was Bethlehem. Bethlehem is a real place in the Middle East.

Here's a picture.

There weren't that many buildings two thousand years ago.

Imagine you were a shepherd just outside of Bethlehem, watching your sheep in the fields at night. Really imagine it.

What does the sky look like? ....

....

What does it smell like? ....

....

Is it warm out or cool? ....

....

What sounds do you hear? ....

....

Now imagine that all of a sudden, a bright light shines around you. And there's an angel there!

What does the angel look like?

....

....

Are you scared? ....

In Luke 2:10-11, the angel says —

"Do not be afraid. I bring you good news. It will bring great joy for all the people. Today in the town of David a Savior has been born to you. He is the Messiah, the Lord."

The angel says you'll find a baby wrapped in cloths and lying in a manger. ← a feeding trough for animals

And then without warning, a huge group of angels shows up saying, "May glory be given to God in the highest heaven! And may peace be given to those He is pleased with on earth!"

If you weren't scared before, you probably are now. And your mind is no doubt capital B, Blown.

When the angels leave, what would you do?

....

....

....

....

....

....

I don't know what you wrote, but I'll tell you what happened in the real story that you can read for yourself in Luke 2. After the angels left, the shepherds ran to Bethlehem to see if they could find a baby in a manger. And they did! They found Jesus with His parents, Mary and Joseph. And then the shepherds did what I think all of us would do if we saw angels from heaven all around us—they told everyone they could find what they had seen. The baby, Jesus, was God's Son and **God sent His Son** to be the Savior to the world.

The shepherds told whomever they could find about what they'd seen.

If angels appeared to you with a message from God, who would be the first person you would tell?

....

DAY 19

Jesus died for you.
(Romans 5:8)

DESCRIBE THE BEST GIFT YOU EVER GOT.

....

....

....

....

....

....

....

....

....

....

The best gift I ever got was a GI Joe command base. It was huge. It had lots of places to set up my action figures and a helipad for my Eaglehawk helicopter. I can play with that thing for hours. I mean I used to play with it. Not anymore. I'm a grown-up. That would be weird.

Do you know who gave the greatest gift ever in the history of the world? God did, when He sent His Son, Jesus. But I'm not sure you understand just how great a gift Jesus was.

Let's test your Jesus knowledge. **Fill in the blanks with the correct word. Choose from the list of words below. You will use each word exactly once.**

Fish	**Samaritan**
Water	**Lazarus**
Life	**Love**
See	**Feet**

1. Jesus could walk anywhere. He even walked on ....

2. Jesus fed 5000 people with just some loaves of bread and a few ....

3. Jesus taught that we should .... our enemies.

4. Jesus brought his friend, ... , back from the dead.

5. Jesus told the parable of The Good ....

6. Jesus spit on a blind man's eyes and he could .... again.

7. Jesus once said, "I am the way and the truth and the ...."

8. Jesus washed his disciples' ....

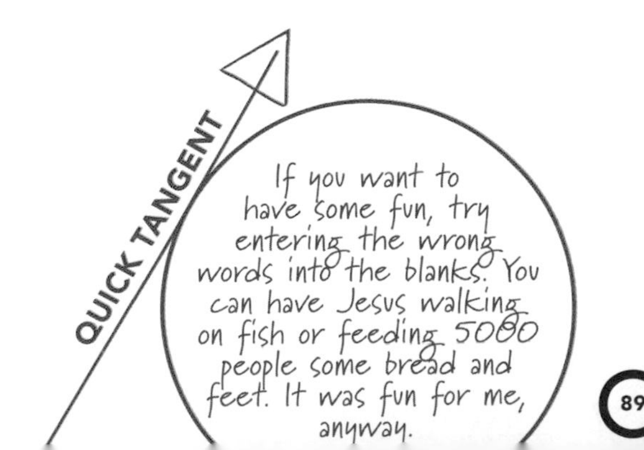

So now you know just a little bit about how great Jesus was. He gave us some wonderful wisdom. He did some amazing things. He loved in ways no one else did.

And then some other things happened.

Jesus was arrested.
Jesus was sentenced to die.
Jesus was nailed to a cross.
Jesus died.

But I don't understand. Jesus was so powerful. He could walk on water and bring people back from the dead. Why did Jesus let himself get arrested? Why did He let himself die?

Romans 5:8 says —

But here is how God has shown his love for us. While we were still sinners, Christ died for us.

Jesus didn't die for nothing. **Jesus died for you.**

Remember we talked about how sin entered the world when Adam and Eve broke God's rule. And they were punished for it. Well, every time you break God's rules, you sin. And someone's got to be punished. Someone's got to pay the price for the broken rules.

Jesus died to pay the price for your sins! He chose to die so that you could be close to God again. Your sins are forgiven because of what Jesus did for you.

WHEN YOU PRAY TONIGHT, ASK GOD TO FORGIVE YOU FOR ANY RULES YOU MIGHT HAVE BROKEN. AND THANK HIM THAT JESUS HAS ALREADY PAID THE PRICE WHEN HE DIED ON THE CROSS FOR YOU.

ANSWERS

1. water, 2. fish, 3. love, 4. Lazarus, 5. Samaritan, 6. see, 7. life, 8. feet

DAY 20

God brought Jesus back from the dead. (Romans 5:10-11)

Why did Jesus have to die? That was the question the disciples must have been asking. Jesus didn't do anything wrong. He loved people. He healed people. He taught people. Someone like that doesn't deserve to be nailed to a cross. But that's what happened. And it was all part of God's plan.

A lot can happen in three days. In three days...

...The earth turns completely around three times.

...You could watch 144 episodes of your favorite half-hour TV show.

...You could read the whole Bible, 16 chapters an hour.

...You could almost clean up your whole room.

On the third day after Jesus was killed, his disciples were in hiding. They feared their lives might be in jeopardy as well. They didn't know what to expect, but they certainly weren't expecting Mary Magdalene to show up with her news.

MARY MAGDALENE: Come quick! They've taken Jesus out of the tomb! We don't know where He is!

PETER: Who has taken Him?

JOHN: Taken Him where?

MARY MAGDALENE: Come and see for yourself.

Peter and John took off running to the tomb to find it was just as Mary said. The stone that blocked the entrance had been rolled away and the tomb where Jesus body should have been was empty. All that was left were the strips of cloth Jesus' body had been wrapped in.

Peter and John left Mary Magdalene outside the tomb. When she looked inside, she saw two angels sitting where Jesus' body had been.

ANGEL: Why are you crying?

MARY MAGDALENE: They've taken Jesus away.

Mary turned around and saw Jesus standing there. But she didn't know it was Jesus. She thought it was the gardener.

Then Jesus said her name.

JESUS: Mary.

And Mary knew at once why Jesus was no longer in the tomb. Jesus was alive! **God brought Jesus back from the dead!**

The disciples would see Jesus with their own eyes later that evening when Jesus somehow appeared to them behind a locked door. And over time, the disciples would finally realize why Jesus had to die.

Romans 5:10-11 says —

Once we were God's enemies. But we have been brought back to him because his Son has died for us. Now that God has brought us back, we are even more secure. We know that we will be saved because Christ lives.

And that is not all.

We are full of joy in God because of our Lord Jesus Christ. Because of him, God has brought us back to himself.

Because of Jesus' death and resurrection, we are finally brought back to God. If we believe in Jesus, we no longer have to be separated from Him. God made you to know Him, and because of Jesus, you can.

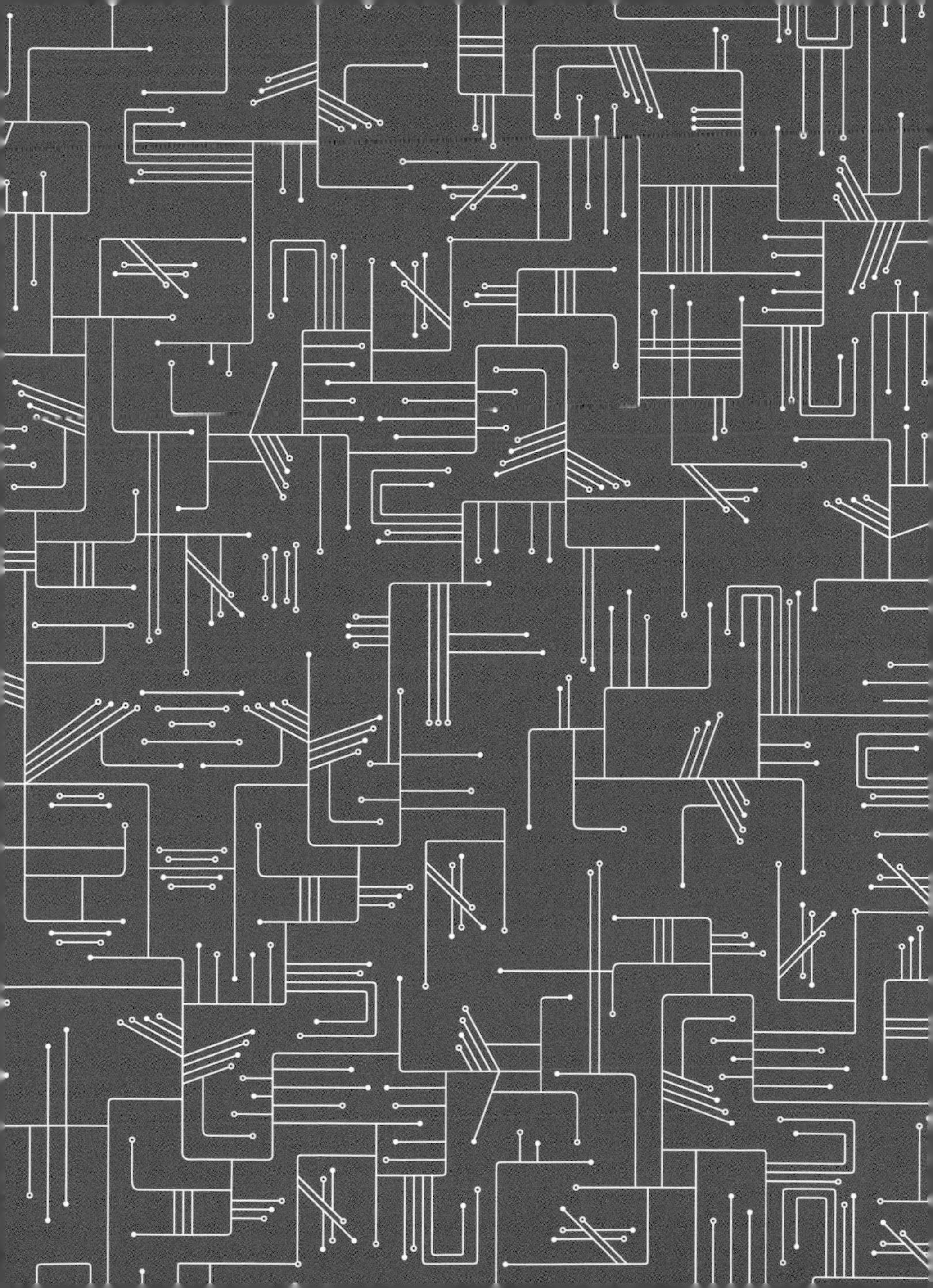

TRY THIS

Break something.

This is going to be the favorite week for some of you. This week you get to break something.

WAIT!!

Don't just go running through your home looking for something to break! You might get in a bit of trouble for that.

Instead, why don't you build something first. Out of LEGOS or Lincoln Logs. Or whatever you have to build with. Build whatever you want. A tower, a castle, a spaceship, a plate of lasagna, whatever.

When you're done, I want you to find a big book, the biggest one in your house. Hold it over the structure you built and drop the book on it.

SMASH!!!

Why in the world would I ask you to do that? Because... breaking things is fun.

Also, because I wanted to remind you that we live in a broken world. When Adam and Eve broke God's rule, everything was broken. Their relationship with God was broken. They could no longer know God the way they were supposed to.

Adam and Eve **SMASHED** their friendship with the Creator of the universe and if it weren't for Jesus, our friendship with God would still be broken.

We should be forever grateful that Jesus died to pay for all the rules we've ever broken and for all the rules we'll ever break.

If you have time, rebuild your tower, or plate of lasagna. This time, don't break it. Put it somewhere safe and let it remind you that your relationship with God is no longer broken.

Even though you'll really want to

WEEK
FIVE

DAY 21

God made you to be you.
(1 Samuel 17:39b-40)

Here's a fun story that you've probably heard. But it never gets old. It's the story of David and Goliath. You can find this story in your Bible in the book of 1 Samuel, chapter 17.

The Philistines and the Israelites were at war. However, the Philistines had a secret weapon: a nine-foot muscle bound soldier named Goliath. He wore armor made of bronze that weighed 125 pounds!

Every day, Goliath would go out on the battlefield and shout, "Choose one of your men! Have him come down and face me! If he wins, we'll surrender. If I win, you have to surrender!"

The only person brave enough to face the giant was a shepherd boy named David.

Before going to the battlefield, King Saul, the leader of the Israelite army, dressed David in a coat of armor that weighed more than David himself! So David said to King Saul: "I can't go out there in all this armor. I'm not used to it."

Have you ever pretended to be someone you're not? I don't mean like in a play. I mean have you ever dressed a certain way, or acted a certain way, or talked a certain way because you thought it would help you fit in?

If you have, you might have felt like David when he tried on the king's armor. He didn't feel comfortable. He didn't feel like himself.

David wanted to face Goliath the way he felt most comfortable. The way God made him.

1 Samuel 17:40 says —

> Then David picked up his wooden staff. He went down to a stream and chose five smooth stones. He put them in the pocket of his shepherd's bag. Then he took his sling in his hand and approached Goliath.

You know what happened next. David went out on the battlefield. He put a stone in his sling, slung it at Goliath and **THWACK!** The giant was defeated.

Would David have defeated the giant if he were wearing all of King Saul's armor? We'll never know. But we do know that God gave David what he needed to win. He gave him faith, courage, and good aim.

God made David to be who he was. And **God made you to be you.** You are one of a kind. You don't have to pretend to be someone you're not. What God has given you is enough.

You probably won't go up against any actual giants in your life. But you may face other kids who tease you because of how you look or act or talk or dress, kids who want you to be more like them. And it will be your decision—be like them or be your own unique self. Which choice would you make?

DAY 22

God knows the real you. (1 Samuel 16:7)

If you could change something about yourself, what would you change?

Would you rather be...

...taller or shorter?
...smarter or stronger?
...older or younger?
...faster or funnier?
...richer or more attractive?

What would happen if you got to be somebody else? Would you be more popular? Would you have more friends to invite to your birthday party? Would you be treated with more respect?

When I was in school, I wanted to be more popular. I wanted to hang out with all the coolest kids in school and talk about what the cool kids talked about. But I was shy and quiet, and people didn't think I was very cool. I always thought that if people could get to know the real me, they would like me.

There's a story in the Bible about a man named Jesse and his eight sons. God told His prophet, Samuel, to choose one of Jesse's sons to be the next king. One by one, Jesse brought his sons to Samuel, each of them tall, strong, and handsome. But they weren't the ones God had chosen.

God told Samuel in 1 Samuel 16:7

"Do not consider how handsome or tall he is. I have not chosen him. The Lord does not look at the things people look at. People look at the outside of a person. But the Lord looks at what is in the heart."

"Do you have any more sons?" asked Samuel.

"My youngest is tending to the sheep," Jesse replied.

Jesse sent for the shepherd, his youngest son, David. God told Samuel to anoint David the next king of Israel, so that's what Samuel did.

Remember him?

"People look at the outside of a person. But the Lord looks at what is in the heart." That means **God knows the real you.** People have the tendency to judge you based on what you look like, what you can do, or how much money you have. God sees past all those things. God sees the real you.

With God, you don't have to pretend to be anything other than yourself. When you pray, you don't have to worry about saying the right words. When you're singing worship songs, you don't have to have the most beautiful voice in the room. When you're reading your Bible, you don't have to understand everything you read. **God knows the real you.** He made you to be you. So with Him, all you have to do is be you.

TAKE A FEW MINUTES TO PRAY. DON'T TRY AND FIND THE PERFECT WORDS. JUST BE YOURSELF. BE HONEST WITH GOD AND TELL HIM WHAT'S TRULY ON YOUR HEART.

DAY 23

God gives you your strength.
(1 Corinthians 12:15-18)

WHAT DO YOU THINK IS THE MOST IMPORTANT PART OF THE HUMAN BODY?

....

WHY?

....

....

....

....

Maybe you said hands are the most important part. You need your hands to do almost anything, play video games, tie your shoes, eat spaghetti. But then, I've seen people eat with their feet before. And without feet, you wouldn't have shoes to tie.

So feet are the most important! You need feet to ride a bike or get from one place to another, or to jump. But then, what good are your feet if you don't have a brain? The brain sends signals to all parts of your body, telling them what to do and where to go.

The brain is the most important part! The brain helps you come up with ideas and solve problems. But then, without the heart pumping all that blood, the brain wouldn't survive.

And how about the lungs giving the body oxygen? Or your ribcage that protects your internal organs? Or your elbows! Why doesn't anybody ever say elbows!?! Have you ever tried doing anything without using your elbows? Try eating an apple. It ain't easy.

So I guess there are a lot of important parts of the body. And many parts rely on the other parts to get their jobs done.

The reason I'm telling you all this is because of something the Bible says. The apostle Paul wrote in a letter to the church in the city of Corinth, "There is one body, but it has many parts. But all its many parts make up one body. It is the same with Christ."

Paul compares people who believe in Jesus to a human body. There are many different kinds of people who make up the body of believers, but together they form the body.

QUICK TANGENT

That reminds me of an old cartoon I used to watch called Voltron, where there were a bunch of these robot cats that would morph together into this one giant robot who would always save the day somehow. You should check it out sometime.

So some people in this body of believers are the hands. Maybe that means they're the servants. The kind of people to whom helping others comes easy.

And some people are the feet. They could be the missionaries. The people who can't wait to travel long distances to do good works for God.

WHAT KIND OF PERSON MIGHT BE A MOUTH?

....

....

HOW ABOUT A BRAIN?

....

....

ELBOW?

....

....

Paul goes on to write that if the body parts could talk, they might argue over where they belong in the body. Maybe the pinky toe would want to try his hand at being, well, a hand. Or the left ear would beg to be in the left foot's shoe... literally.

But here's what 1 Corinthians 12:18 says —

God has placed each part in the body just as He wanted it to be.

You belong to the body of believers. God gives you your strengths—the strengths you need to play your unique role in that body. You can know that God has put you exactly where He wants you to be. Your strengths may be different than all the other parts of the body, but that doesn't mean you aren't where you belong.

WHICH PART OF THE BODY DO YOU THINK YOU WOULD BE?

....

WHY?

....

....

....

DAY 24

God knows what you need.
(Matthew 6:8b)

The body parts below are missing some letters. See if you can give them the letters they need. If you need help, see the answers at the bottom of the next page.

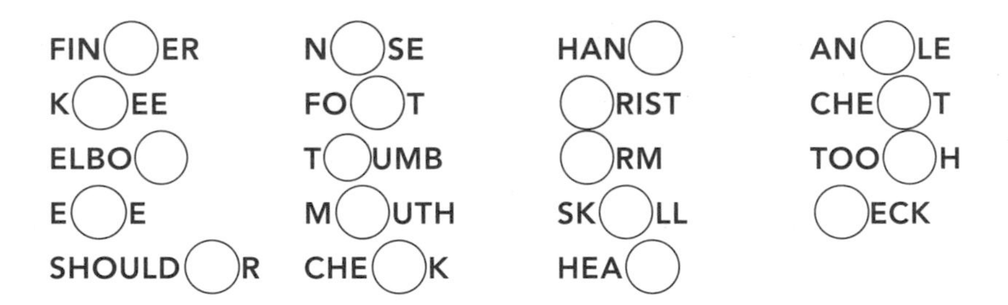

Read the letters you wrote from left to right to reveal a hidden message.

If you got all the right answers, it should read God knows what you need.

And it's true. God knows everything. He made you. He knows you inside and out. He knows you better than you know yourself.

Jesus said in Matthew 6:8 —

"Your Father knows what you need even before you ask him."

QUICK TANGENT

If God knows what I need before I ask Him, that must mean He knows what I'm thinking. So if I start thinking about monkeys tap dancing on the moon, God will know. Now I really am thinking about monkeys tap dancing on the moon. Sorry, God.

ANSWERS

finger
knee
elbow
eye
shoulder
nose
foot
thumb
mouth
cheek
hand
wrist
arm
skull
head
ankle
chest
tooth
neck

It's good that God knows what we need, because sometimes we don't even know what we need. We know what we want, sure. But what we need is sometimes a different story.

Take my friend, Brad, for example. Brad really wanted a pet giraffe. So he prayed every night.

"God, please let me have a pet giraffe. I love giraffes and know all about them. I've even bought a stepladder to help me feed him. I really need this giraffe. Amen."

Did God hear Brad's prayers? Sure, He did! God always listens to our prayers. But that doesn't mean Brad ended up with a pet giraffe. Maybe it's because God knew what Brad didn't know. Brad couldn't afford a giraffe. He would need at least $50,000. Also, Brad lived in an apartment and the giraffe would have never fit in the elevator. Brad needed to live on a wildlife preserve if he wanted to have a pet giraffe.

I have a confession to make. I don't have a friend named Brad. I made that story up. But the idea is still the same. We know what we want, but we don't always know what we need. **God knows what you need.** So if you've ever wondered why God doesn't answer certain prayers the way you want or expect, it could be because He knows what you need better than you do.

NEXT TIME YOU PRAY, ASK GOD FOR WHAT YOU NEED, BUT PRAY KNOWING THAT HE ALREADY KNOWS. ASK HIM TO HELP YOU KNOW WHAT YOU REALLY NEED AND NOT JUST WHAT YOU WANT.

DAY 25

God knows your whole story. (Psalm 139:16)

IT'S TIME TO WRITE YOUR AUTOBIOGRAPHY. AN AUTOBIOGRAPHY IS A TRUE STORY THAT'S ALL ABOUT YOU. I'LL START, AND YOU FILL IN THE BLANKS.

My name is ....

I was born on ....

The first city I lived in was ....

My first memory is ....

....

....

....

....

....

My favorite thing in the whole world is ....

....

....

....

....

That'll get you started. It's good to write an autobiography or keep a journal about yourself, because nobody knows you better than you. Well, almost nobody...

God knows you. He knows you even better than you know yourself. He made you. He gives you your strengths. He knows you inside and outside. He knows your beginning.

"You created the deepest parts of my being. You put me together inside my mother's body."

Psalm 139:13

And He knows how your story will end.

Psalm 139:16 says —

You planned how many days I would live. You wrote down the number of them in your book before I had lived through even one of them.

God knows your whole story. The beginning, the end, and everything in between. He can already see the problems you're going to have, the mistakes you're going to make, and the presents you'll get for Christmas this year. God knows everything about you!

ANSWER THESE QUESTIONS ABOUT YOUR FUTURE.

What are you going to be when you grow up?

....

What city will you live in?

....

Are you going to get married?

....

Have children?

....

What kind of car will you drive?

....

If you don't know the answers to those questions, that's okay. You're not supposed to. Even though you may know what you *want* the answers to those questions to be, you can't predict the future. But God knows the answers to those questions. **God knows your whole story.**

And you know what else? Your story is not like anyone else's story. Sure, there will be some things about you that will be the same as somebody else. But no one will live the exact same story as you will. And that's a good thing, because it means you'll have a unique perspective on the world. You'll look at things in ways no one else will. You'll have solutions to problems that no one else can find. You'll be able to communicate with people in unique ways. God made you in such a way that you and only you can do the things you do.

KEEP ALL THAT IN MIND WHEN YOU'RE WRITING THAT AUTOBIOGRAPHY OF YOURS.

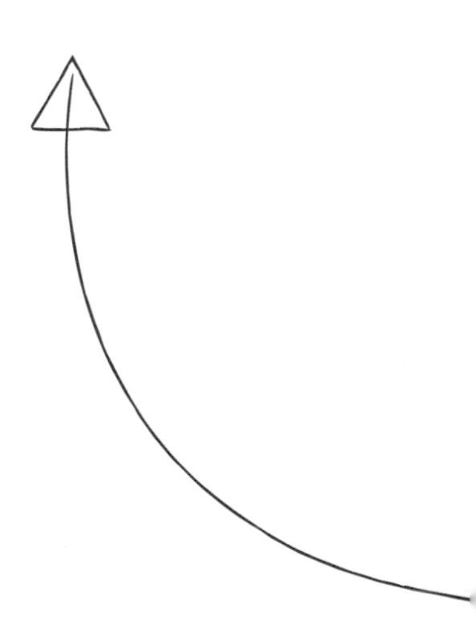

TRY THIS

Remember something.

You should have gotten a good start on your autobiography by now, but how about we dig a little deeper. God made you to be you, so I want you to write a story about yourself. A true story. Something that really happened to you. It doesn't have to be a long story. I won't be checking it to make sure all the words are spelled correctly. I just want it to be an honest story that only you can tell. Because believe it or not, no one remembers how things happened in your life the same way you remember them.

I'll tell you a true story from my life to help get you thinking.

> **One day not too long ago, I was walking in the woods along a trail when it started to rain . . . hard. I hurried to find shelter when I came to a bridge that was supposed to cross over a stream. But with the rain, the stream was crossing over the bridge. The only way to get across without getting wet was to walk on the rails of the bridge, kind of like walking a balance beam. I made it halfway across before my foot slipped and I fell into the water. My first thought as I came up for air was, "I hope nobody saw that." And then, you know, I was happy that I was alive. I made it safely to shelter after that, but I was more than a little bit wet.**

It's that simple. All you have to do is remember something that happened and write it down. Then you'll have it here forever. Okay, go.

Your stories are what make you who you are. So it's good to remember them. There are things that have happened to you that you think you'll remember forever, but I promise you, unless you write them down, they'll slip away from your memory as you get older. So keep track of your stories. Keep a record of the things that happen and the things God does for you. You'll thank me later.

WEEK SIX

DAY 26

God made you for an adventure.
(Genesis 12)

When I was a kid, I loved adventure movies. But especially movies with Indiana Jones. Indiana Jones was an archaeologist/explorer who was always on the hunt for artifacts and treasures. He traveled all over the world getting into and out of tough situations. Oh, how I wished I could be Indiana Jones.

IF YOU COULD BE AN ADVENTURER OR MOVIE HERO, WHO WOULD YOU RATHER BE?

Indiana Jones	**Moana**	**Katniss**
Iron Man	**Captain America**	**Han Solo**
Black Widow	**Sherlock Holmes**	**Tarzan**
Lara Croft	**Kung Fu Panda**	**Rey**
The Hulk	**Spider-Man**	**Batman**
Luke Skywalker	**Wonder Woman**	**Mowgli**

SOMEBODY ELSE?

....

....

WHERE WOULD YOU WANT YOUR ADVENTURE TO HAPPEN?

The jungle
Outer space
Your backyard
The ocean
New York City
The mountains
Rio de Janeiro
Antarctica
Egypt
China
London
Bombay

SOME PLACE ELSE?

....

....

WHAT WOULD YOU LIKE TO DO WHEN YOU GOT THERE?

Solve mysteries
Find hidden treasure
Explore new places
Eat exotic food
Make money
Bungee jump
Save lives
Have fun

SOMETHING ELSE?

....

....

....

....

....

The Bible tells the story of another adventurer. A guy who didn't even know he was going on an adventure. A guy named Abram.

Abram lived thousands of years ago in a place called Harran. There was nothing particularly special about Abram, not that we know of anyway. All we know is that God chose Abram for a very special purpose.

In Genesis 12, you can read the first part of Abram's epic adventure.

In the first verse, God says to Abram —

"Go from your country, your people and your father's family. Go to the land I will show you."

Then God promised to make Abram into a great nation, and told Abram that all nations on earth would be blessed because of him.

God told Abram to go, so... Abram went. That's it. He didn't complain to God about not having enough information. He didn't make excuses about how hard it was going to be to move his whole family to who knows where. Abram went. And his adventure with God began.

Here's something that may surprise you. **God made you for an adventure.** God has a plan for your life. Someday, God may want you to go somewhere or do something for Him. It could be a mission trip to help people in need. It could be as simple as telling someone about Jesus. It could be something you don't fully understand. Will you make excuses, or will you do like Abram did and go?

THAT'S A HARD QUESTION TO ANSWER WHEN YOU DON'T EVEN KNOW WHAT YOUR ADVENTURE IS GOING TO BE. SO TAKE A FEW MINUTES RIGHT NOW TO ASK GOD TO PREPARE YOU FOR WHATEVER ADVENTURE HE'S GOT IN STORE FOR YOU.

DAY 27

You're never too small for an adventure. (Judges 6:15-16)

Have you ever been told, "You're not old enough"? Whether it's rides at the fair or an especially gory Marvel movie, it probably feels like you will always be too young for the really fun stuff. List three things you wish you were old enough for here:

1. ....

2. ....

3. ....

You might not think you're old enough to go on an adventure. You might think that God would never use someone like you.

Well, consider the story of Gideon. You can read his story in the book of Judges, chapters 6 and 7.

Gideon was an Israelite. The Israelites were in a bit of trouble. For seven years, they were tormented by the Midianites. The Israelites would plant their crops and the Midianites would come and destroy the crops, leaving the Israelites with virtually nothing. So the Israelites cried out to God for help.

CUE THE ADVENTURE MUSIC!

That's when God called on Gideon. Gideon, faster than a speeding gazelle, more powerful than a hurricane, able to defeat an entire army with just his pinky! Gideon would save the day!!!

WAIT! STOP THE MUSIC!

That's not who Gideon was at all. Gideon wasn't some superhero. He was just a guy. In fact, when God sent his angel to recruit Gideon for the job, Gideon replied, "My family group is the weakest in the tribe of Manasseh. And I'm the least important member of my family."

If that's true, Gideon is the last person God should be calling on to help the Israelites. God should find someone bigger and more important. Someone who will make the Midianites shake in their boots.

Nope. God chose Gideon.

And God tells Gideon in Judges 6:16 —

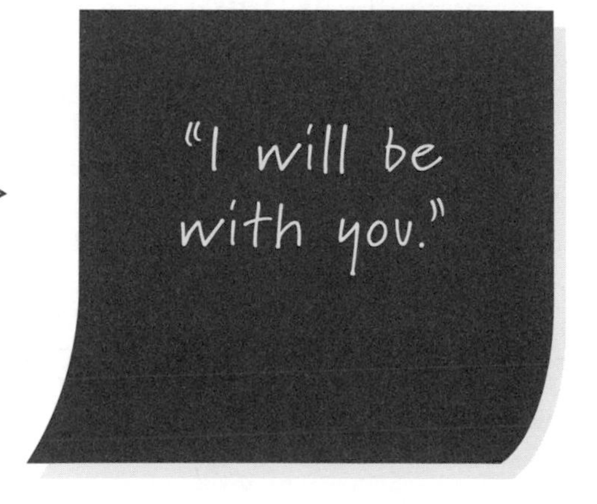

Well, that's a different story, isn't it? With the all-powerful Creator of the universe with him, Gideon is sure to succeed! And he did! With only 300 men in his army, Gideon defeated over 100,000 Midianites!

and God

It kind of makes you wonder, though. Why would God choose the least important family member of the weakest tribe to go on His adventure? I think it's so God gets all the glory He deserves. If He had used a ginormous hero with super strength, people would give the hero all the credit. Instead God used the small dude, so God gets the credit.

How tall are you?

....

How much do you weigh?

....

Scratch out the answers you wrote and write, '**BIG ENOUGH!**' Because no matter how big or how small you are, you're **BIG ENOUGH** to be used by God. **You're never too small for an adventure.**

God can use you the way He used Gideon. Maybe not to defeat an army. But He's God! Who knows what adventure He might have for you?

YOU MAY ALREADY BE ON YOUR ADVENTURE. OR MAYBE YOUR ADVENTURE IS COMING SOON. IN ANY CASE, BE ON THE LOOKOUT FOR GOD TO USE YOU IN SOME BIG WAYS.

DAY 28

Choose the right adventure.
(Proverbs 22:3)

When I was younger, I read a series of books called *Choose Your Own Adventure*. In these books, you would read an adventure story and at the end of some of the pages you'd have a choice to make. Turn to page 10 if you want to go down the dark and scary tunnel. Turn to page 17 if you choose the creepy twisting pathway.

Why am I telling you about it? I'll show you!

The following story is told *Choose Your Own Adventure* style. Follow the directions and hopefully you'll make it to the end safely. Choose wisely.

Hello brave explorer! Welcome to the rain forests of Borneo! You've traveled all this way to find a rare species of butterfly – the Trogonoptera brooking, or as you've nicknamed it – Troggy. You have your butterfly net, a flashlight, and your trusty Polaroid camera. What could possibly go wrong?

Hisssssssss. **You turn to see one of the largest snakes you could ever imagine. A Borneo python if you had to guess.**

- If you want to go in for a closer look and a photograph, go to paragraph A.
- If you want to stay still like a tree, go to paragraph B.
- If you want to run, go to paragraph C.

A – You walk slowly toward the snake, camera in hand. You're close enough to touch it now. You were right! It is a Borneo python. You could tell all your friends how right you were. If only the python wasn't eating you. *YOUR ADVENTURE IS OVER!*

B – The snake slithers closer to you as you stand as still as a statue. It doesn't seem to realize you're potentially food. It's possible, however, that you're a little too convincing as a tree, because the snake is starting to climb up your leg.

- If you want to keep pretending to be a tree and see what happens, go to paragraph D.
- If you want to shake the snake off and run, go to paragraph C.

C – You start running. You hear the snap of the snake's jaws behind you as you gallop away. You escaped! You slow down as you see the entrance to a dark foreboding cave. There's no need for you to look for Troggy in there. But the cave does make you curious.

- If you want to go into the dark cave, go to paragraph E.
- If you want to keep looking for Troggy, go to paragraph F.

D – The snake makes its way up to your arms, the "branches" of your pretend tree. The snake coils around you and gets comfy. It's taking a nap! Now all you have to do is stand completely still until the snake wakes up. Too bad you feel that sneeze coming on. Ah...ah...ah... CHOO! *YOUR ADVENTURE IS OVER!*

E – You turn on your flashlight and enter the cave. Nope. No butterflies here. There are, however, a swarm of bats. They don't like your flashlight much. The last thing you hear is the flutter of a thousand wings. *YOUR ADVENTURE IS OVER!*

F – You walk down a slightly overgrown path for several minutes when you see it! Right in front of you. Troggy! Resting on a leaf. You snap a quick picture with your camera. The folks back home are going to be so jealous. *YOU HAVE SUCCEEDED!*

You know, life is kind of like a *Choose Your Own Adventure* book. We face choices every single day. Some are wise, some are unwise. And if you're honest, most of the time you can tell the difference between what is wise and what is unwise.

Proverbs 22:3 says —

Wise people see danger and go to a safe place. But childish people keep going and suffer for it.

It's important to **choose the right adventure** in your life. Choose the wise adventure. Don't do things that you know are unsafe or unwise.

WHEN YOU PRAY, ASK GOD TO HELP YOU KNOW THE DIFFERENCE BETWEEN WHAT IS WISE AND WHAT IS UNWISE. YOUR BIBLE CAN HELP, TOO, SO KEEP READING IT. YOU DON'T WANT YOUR ADVENTURE TO END TOO SOON, BRAVE EXPLORER!

DAY 29

Don't be afraid of adventure. (Joshua 1:9)

What are you afraid of? Is it the dark? Or snakes? Is it being in a crowded place? Or are you afraid of heights? There are a lot of things people are afraid of. There's a word for it. Being afraid of something is called a phobia.

SEE IF YOU CAN MATCH EACH PHOBIA WITH ITS DEFINITION. THE ANSWERS ARE AT THE BOTTOM OF THE NEXT PAGE.

1. Arachnophobia
2. Claustrophobia
3. Astraphobia
4. Aerophobia
5. Trypophobia
6. Alektorophobia
7. Hippopotomonstroses-quippedaliophobia
8. Triskaidekaphobia

a. Fear of thunder and lightning
b. Fear of holes
c. Fear of long words
d. Fear of spiders
e. Fear of flying
f. Fear of small spaces
g. Fear of chickens
h. Fear of the number 13

So there are a lot of things to be afraid of. I think after reading those phobias, I've found some new things to be afraid of. Chickens do sort of creep me out.

But there's one thing you shouldn't be afraid of. **Don't be afraid of adventure.** God made you for an adventure after all. Now I don't know what adventure you're on right now. Your family could be moving from one home to another. Maybe you just welcomed a new baby brother or sister into your home. Or maybe your next adventure will be the fourth grade. I don't know.

I do know this. Whatever your adventure, you aren't alone.

There's a guy in the Bible named Joshua. He's got a whole book named after him in the Old Testament. After Moses led the Israelites out of slavery in Egypt, Joshua was one of God's most faithful followers. So faithful, in fact, that when Moses died, God put Joshua in charge. Now there's something to be afraid of. Being the leader of thousands of people who are looking to you to decide where they go and what they do. What if you mess up?

Fear of failure = atychiphobia

But God spoke to Joshua directly.

In Joshua 1:9, God told Joshua —

"Here is what I am commanding you to do. Be strong and brave. Do not be afraid. Do not lose hope. I am the Lord your God. I will be with you everywhere you go."

Fear of loud noises = Ligyrophobia

QUICK TANGENT

Wow! I wish God would talk to me like that. That way I would know for sure He was there with me. Then again, a voice out of nowhere might terrify me. Great, now I have something to add to my list of phobias.

ANSWERS
1d, 2f, 3a, 4e,
5b, 6g, 7c, 8h

Joshua had faith that God would be with him, and with God on his side, Joshua won many battles for the Israelites.

Here's why that matters to you. When you're following God's will, when you're on one of His adventures, God is on your side, too. There's no need to fear when God is with you.

THINK ABOUT SOME OF THE THINGS YOU'RE AFRAID OF, THE DARK, HEIGHTS, CHICKENS. ASK GOD TO HELP YOU BE BRAVE WHEN FACING THOSE FEARS. AND IF YOU FIND YOURSELF ON ONE OF GOD'S ADVENTURES, HAVE FAITH THAT HE IS RIGHT THERE WITH YOU.

DAY 30

You don't always choose your adventure.
(Genesis 50:20)

WHAT'S THE CRAZIEST DREAM YOU EVER HAD?

....

....

....

....

....

....

....

....

....

....

....

QUICK TANGENT

In my craziest dream, I'm on a boat with the snowman from the old Rudolph, the Red-Nosed Reindeer cartoon and we're actually floating on a sea of gummi worms. The snowman says, 'Go ahead. Dive in.' And so I jump off the boat. That's when I wake up. And I'm hungry for gummi worms.

Some people think our dreams have meanings. One of those people is a guy from the Bible named Joseph. Joseph's adventure can be found in the book of Genesis, chapter 37, and 39 through 50. Imagine Joseph's life is like a roller coaster with high points and low points. The roller coaster starts out climbing.

Joseph had big dreams about his future. Dreams where he was an important leader, and his family was bowing down to him. These dreams made his brothers jealous. The roller coaster reaches its first hill and plummets! Joseph's brothers were so jealous, they beat him up, threw him down a well, then sold him into slavery, making their father believe Joseph was dead!

He had 11 bros!

But even though Joseph was sold as a slave to an Egyptian named Potiphar, the Bible says that the Lord was with Joseph. The roller coaster starts another climb. Joseph became Potiphar's favorite servant and he was placed in charge of the whole house.

But then . . . another downhill plummet! Joseph was accused of a crime he didn't commit and he was thrown in prison.

Yet even in prison, the Bible says the Lord was with Joseph. The roller coaster climbs. Joseph was such a model prisoner, the man running the prison put Joseph in charge of all the prisoners.

Still climbing... Two of the prisoners Joseph was in charge of used to work closely with the Pharaoh. God helped Joseph interpret their dreams and they promised to remember Joseph if they ever got out of prison. The dreams came true, but Joseph was forgotten. The roller coaster falls hitting an all-time low. Joseph's future was definitely not going as planned.

You don't always choose your adventure. Sometimes you have great plans for your future, even pure unselfish plans, but God takes you in a different direction. He takes you out of your comfort zone. Sometimes it might feel like a roller coaster with ups and downs and twists and turns.

Two years later, Pharaoh had a dream. Finally, Joseph was remembered and God helped him interpret Pharaoh's dream. Pharaoh was so pleased, Joseph was made second in command of all of Egypt. And through his efforts, Joseph helped get the country through a terrible famine.

When Joseph came face to face with his brothers again, they bowed down to him, just as Joseph dreamed they would. They were afraid of what Joseph might do to them. But Joseph said, in Genesis 50:20 —

"You planned to harm me. But God planned it for good. He planned to do what is now being done. He wanted to save many lives."

Even when you don't choose your adventure, when things don't go the way you want or expect, remember that God's plan is bigger and better than your own. Think about your own life as a roller coaster.

What are some high points?

....

....

....

....

What are some low points?

....

....

....

....

WHATEVER YOU WROTE, OR WHATEVER HAPPENS IN YOUR LIFE, HIGH OR LOW, GOD CAN USE IT FOR GOOD.

TRY THIS

Explore something.

In the book of Genesis, God asked Abram to go somewhere he'd never been before. And Abram went. I expect Abram was a little afraid of the road ahead, but possibly he was excited, too. It can be fun to explore new things and new places. It can be an adventure.

So try this. Explore something. Some place you've never really explored. Start in your own home.

Now hold on a second. Don't go looking for your older sister's diary. You know well enough what's off limits to you.

Instead, look closely at things you've never looked closely at before. Use a magnifying glass if you've got one. Look at those old pictures of your parents. Look at the knick-knacks gathering dust on the mantel. Look at the dust bunnies underneath your sofa. Ask questions about things you don't recognize.

If you have an attic or a basement, you can get permission to explore there. Or the dark closet at the end of the hall.

A big part of adventuring is being observant. You never know what sort of things you'll find.

Write down some of the things you discovered while you were exploring.

God made you for an adventure. And chances are, you won't hear God talking to you the way Abram did. So you have to keep your eyes and ears open. Be observant and look for ways God wants to use you on His adventure.

WEEK SEVEN

DAY 31

God made you to follow Jesus. (Acts 8:34-35)

Here we go. Time for another recap. You can help. Circle the words that make each sentence correct.

1. In the beginning, God *created* / *destroyed* everything.
2. God made a man and woman named Adam and *Elizabeth* / *Eve*.
3. They broke God's rule when they ate *fruit* / *spaghetti* from the tree of the knowledge of good and evil.
4. When sin entered the world, people were *closer to* / *separated from* God.
5. God promised to send a *giant robot* / *Savior* to bring us back to Him.
6. Jesus died on a cross to pay for our *sins* / *mistakes*.
7. God brought Jesus back from *the dead* / *Albuquerque*.

The book of Acts tells us what happened after that. It tells the story of what the apostles said and did after they saw Jesus alive again.

The word apostle comes from a Greek word that means messenger. And that's just what the apostles were. They were messengers, spreading the good news about Jesus to as many people as they could.

One of those messengers was Philip. One day, the Bible says, an angel of the Lord spoke to Philip and told him to go south to the desert road. On his way, Philip came upon an important official from Ethiopia riding in a chariot.

The Holy Spirit told Philip to get close to the chariot, so that's what Philip did.

When Philip got close to the chariot, he overheard the Ethiopian official reading from the book of Isaiah. Though it probably wasn't a book back then, but rather a scroll.

"Do you understand what you're reading?" Philip asked. The Ethiopian official replied, "No. Can you explain it to me?" And he invited Philip to join him in the chariot.

The official was reading a passage from Isaiah that told about the coming Messiah, and how He would die.

Acts 8:34 and 35 say —

The official said to Philip, "Tell me, please. Who is the prophet talking about? Himself, or someone else?" Then Philip began with that same part of Scripture. He told him the good news about Jesus.

My guess is that Philip also told the official about all the things we discussed in the recap above. How God made everything, and how we were separated from God when sin entered the world, and how Jesus' death and resurrection brought us back to Him.

Philip wanted the Ethiopian official to understand what he was made for. That God made him to follow Jesus. And if Philip were sitting next to you today, he would want you to know the same thing. **God made you to follow Jesus.** That's what God's big story is all about.

When he found out about Jesus, the Ethiopian official asked to be baptized. And after the baptism, the Bible says the Spirit of the Lord suddenly took Philip away. I guess he was pretty fast.

Just like He made the Ethiopian official, **God made you to follow Jesus.** But what does it mean to follow Jesus? Is Jesus really worth following? And where can you find a spaghetti tree? All great questions—most of which will be answered as you read on this week.

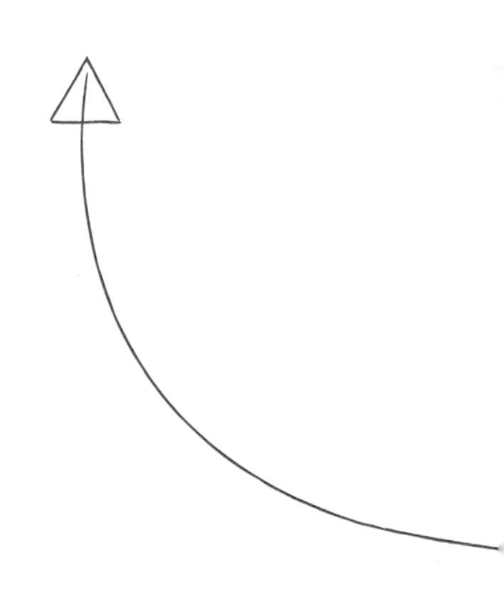

DAY 32

Jesus is wise.
(Mathew 7:24)

Here's a question. Why should you follow Jesus? You might have several different answers to that question.

...Because the Bible says so
...Because God wants me to
...Because my parents told me to

Those are all good answers. But what is it about Jesus that makes Him worth following? Again, there are **SO** many things. He's powerful, He's compassionate, He's the Son of God, He loved you enough to give His life for you. There are plenty of reasons to follow Jesus.

And here's another. **Jesus is wise.** If you read the Gospels, you'll find that what Jesus said was always chock full of wisdom.

Matthew, Mark, Luke, and John

SEE IF YOU CAN MATCH THE WISDOM WITH THE PERSON WHO SAID IT.

1. "So don't worry about tomorrow.
2. Tomorrow will worry about itself.
3. Each day has enough trouble of its own."
4. "Here is what I tell you. Love your enemies. Pray for those who hurt you."
5. "When you give to needy people, don't let your left hand know what your right hand is doing."
6. "If a kingdom fights against itself, it can't stand."
7. "Those who are healthy don't need a doctor. Sick people do."
8. "What good is it if someone gains the whole world but loses their soul?"

A. Jesus

B. Jesus

C. Jesus

D. Jesus

E. Jesus

F. Jesus

G. Jesus

H. Jesus

Okay, so that was a pretty easy quiz. Jesus said all those things. But if you really want to follow Jesus, there's more to it than just knowing what He said.

Jesus told a parable about wise and foolish builders. In Matthew 7:24, Jesus said —

"So then, everyone who hears my words and puts them into practice is like a wise man. He builds his house on the rock."

And anyone who hears Jesus' words and doesn't put them into practice is like a foolish man who builds his house on the sand.

Which house do you think has a better chance outlasting a storm?

....

Hopefully you said the wise man's house. His house will stand up to the storm. The other house? **KABLOOEY!**

Jesus is wise. So it only makes sense that when you follow Jesus and DO what Jesus says to do, you will be wise, too. Not only that, you'll be more able to stand up to any storms that might come your way.

THINK ABOUT ANY STORMS YOU MIGHT HAVE IN YOUR LIFE RIGHT NOW. TROUBLE AT HOME OR WITH A FRIEND, TROUBLE AT SCHOOL OR SOMETHING YOU CAN'T EVEN EXPLAIN. HOPEFULLY YOUR LIFE IS STORM FREE, BUT NO MATTER WHAT, ASK GOD TO HELP YOU STAY STRONG BY FOLLOWING JESUS.

DAY 33

Jesus is powerful.
(John 11:43-44)

Jesus is wise. And when you follow Him by hearing and doing what He says, you can withstand any storm. But in case you need another great reason to follow Jesus, **He is also powerful.** Like, *really* powerful.

Jesus wasn't just a wise teacher, although that was a very important part of His ministry. He was also incredibly powerful. I'll bet the disciples used to hang out swapping stories about the stuff Jesus did.

> **BARTHOLOMEW:** Ooh! Remember that time we were out on the boat and we had that storm. We thought we were gonna die! And Jesus was just back there sleeping! So we woke Him up and Jesus waved His hand and the storm just . . . stopped. It just stopped!
>
> **PETER:** Oh! Oh! And remember when it was time to pay taxes, Jesus told me to go out to the lake and catch a fish. And the first fish I caught had a coin inside it, the exact amount we needed to pay taxes!
>
> **JAMES:** Or that time He saw the fig tree without figs on it. Jesus told that tree never to bear fruit again and the tree dried up almost immediately.
>
> **JOHN:** What about Lazarus!

They probably told the story of Lazarus over and over again. Lazarus was Jesus' friend. And Lazarus got very sick. Lazarus' sisters knew how powerful Jesus was, so they sent for Him immediately hoping Jesus could heal their brother.

Jesus took his time, however. He said, "This sickness will not end in death. No, it is for God's glory. God's Son will receive glory because of it." But Jesus was too late, or so everyone thought. Lazarus died. And by the time Jesus got there, Lazarus had been buried for four days.

These people knew Jesus was powerful. They'd seen all the things He could do, but four days in the grave? Surely Jesus couldn't do anything about that. When you're dead, you're dead. But time and time again, when you read the story of Jesus, He finds new ways to surprise you.

Jesus came up to Lazarus' tomb. He looked up and prayed.

Then, John 11:43 and 44 say —

> Jesus called in a loud voice. He said, "Lazarus, come out!" The dead man came out. His hands and feet were wrapped with strips of linen. A cloth was around his face. Jesus said to them, "Take off the clothes he was buried in and let him go."

WHAT? Can you believe that? The man was buried for four days! And Jesus says three words, "Lazarus, come out!" And he comes out! **ALIVE!!!** I'm going to say it again.
Jesus is powerful!

He has power over the weather, over animals, over nature! He has power over death itself! There is truly nothing that Jesus can't do! That is a very good reason to follow Him.

WHEN YOU PRAY, THINK ABOUT HOW POWERFUL JESUS IS. TELL HIM THAT YOU RECOGNIZE HOW AMAZING HE IS AND THAT YOU KNOW HE HAS EVERYTHING UNDER HIS CONTROL.

DAY 34

Jesus is compassionate. (Matthew 20:34)

We know Jesus is wise, and we know Jesus is powerful. But there's still another reason to follow Jesus. (And since there's one more day to this devotional week, it's probably safe to assume I'm not out of reasons yet.)

Jesus is compassionate. What does it mean to be compassionate? Maybe you know already. **I'll give you some scenarios and you tell me what a compassionate person would do.**

1. Four friends are playing volleyball on the beach. One of the friends gets hit right in the nose by the volleyball. There's only a little blood, but the friend looks a bit dizzy. **What would a compassionate person do for this dizzy friend?**

....

....

....

2. A boy's dog just died after living a long, incredibly fun life. The boy is very sad because he misses his friend. **What would a compassionate person do for this sad boy?**

....

....

....

3. Despite studying very hard for her history test, a girl gets a failing grade. If she doesn't get a better grade on the make-up test, she might fail the class altogether. **What would a compassionate person do for this girl?**

....

....

....

Sometimes it's hard to know what to do when someone is hurting or sad or struggling. Being compassionate means you feel or show concern for someone in those situations. Maybe that means stopping to help someone out. Maybe it means just being there. Maybe it means praying to God for help.

The Bible is full of stories about Jesus' compassion for others. When He stopped to heal someone. When He was patient enough to answer someone's question. When He helped a friend who was hurting.

One of those stories is of two blind men who were sitting by a road that Jesus was passing. Jesus was followed by a large crowd. The blind men shouted, "Lord! Son of David! Have mercy on us!"

The crowd tried to silence the two men, but they shouted even louder, "**LORD! SON OF DAVID! HAVE MERCY ON US!**"

Jesus asked them, "What do you want me to do for you?"

"We want to see," they answered.

Jesus didn't have to help these two men. They weren't particularly special. We don't even know their names. But **Jesus is compassionate**, and Jesus is powerful, so . . .

Matthew 20:34 says —

Jesus felt deep concern for them. He touched their eyes. Right away they could see. And they followed him.

You probably aren't able to be compassionate in the way Jesus is. He's too powerful. But when you follow Him, it will hopefully give you a heart for those who are suffering or in pain.

TALK TO GOD. IF ANYTHING IS TROUBLING YOU, TELL HIM ABOUT IT. KNOW THAT HE WILL LISTEN AND HAVE COMPASSION NO MATTER WHAT YOU'RE GOING THROUGH.

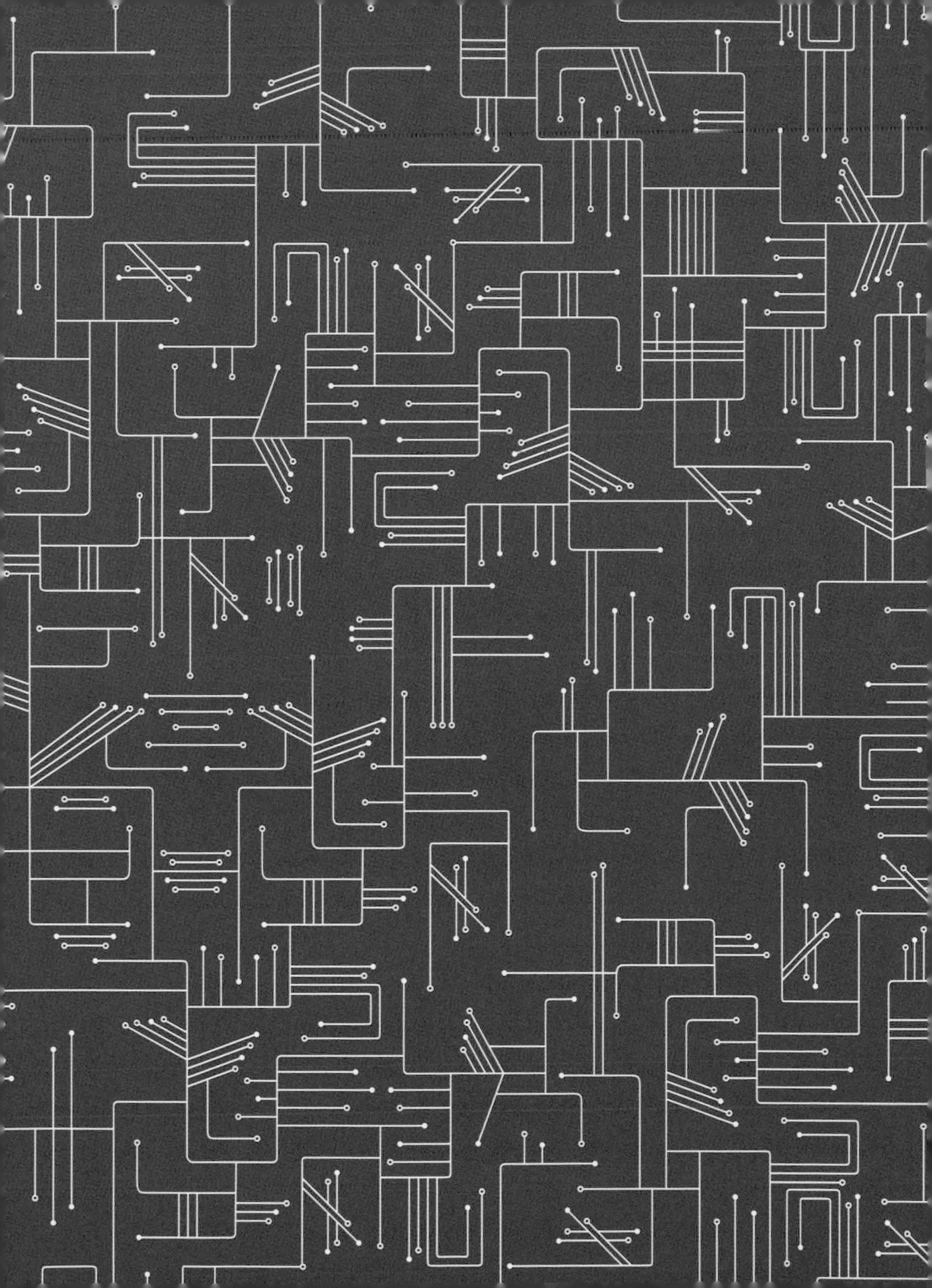

DAY 35

**Jesus loves you.
(John 15:13)**

RATE HOW MUCH YOU LOVE THE FOLLOWING THINGS FROM 1 TO 10.

Pizza	1	2	3	4	5	6	7	8	9	10
Ice Cream	1	2	3	4	5	6	7	8	9	10
Jigsaw Puzzles	1	2	3	4	5	6	7	8	9	10
Horses	1	2	3	4	5	6	7	8	9	10
Cars	1	2	3	4	5	6	7	8	9	10
Video Games	1	2	3	4	5	6	7	8	9	10
Clothes	1	2	3	4	5	6	7	8	9	10
Chocolate	1	2	3	4	5	6	7	8	9	10
Your Parents	1	2	3	4	5	6	7	8	9	10
Your Best Friend	1	2	3	4	5	6	7	8	9	10

QUICK TANGENT

I rated chocolate higher than my best friend. Does that make me a bad person?

We love a lot of different things and different people, but I'll bet you don't love anything as much as **Jesus loves you.** God made you to follow Jesus. Jesus is wise, powerful, and compassionate. But one of the greatest reasons to follow Him is that **Jesus loves you.**

Jesus loves you. This I know. For the Bible tells me so.

Let's talk about how much Jesus loves you.

In John 15:13, Jesus says —

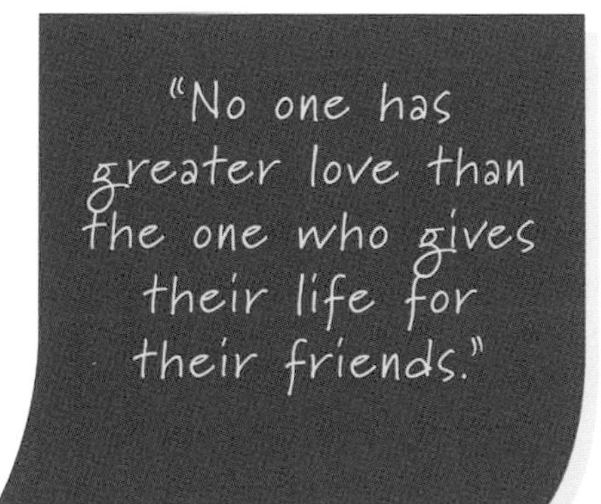

And Jesus did give up His life for His friends. He gave up His life for you. But He didn't have to. He had lots of opportunities to escape.

When Jesus was arrested, His captors all fell to the ground when Jesus announced, "I am He!" But Jesus didn't run.

Jesus' disciples tried to fight back. Peter even cut off one of the servant's ears. Jesus told Peter to put his sword away. Jesus didn't fight.

And not only that, remember, Jesus is powerful. At any moment, He could have called down angels to rescue Him from the cross. But Jesus didn't call for help.

No. Jesus died, because He knew you couldn't pay the price for your sin on your own. He chose not to run, not to fight, and not to call for help, because He loves you that much.

So how much does Jesus love you on a scale from 1 to 10?

1 2 3 4 5 6 7 8 9 10

Circle the 10. Put a star on it! Point arrows at it! Add a bunch of zeroes to it! Because **Jesus loves you** more than you can count. He is on your side, always. And that's another great reason to follow Him.

YOU LEARNED THIS WEEK THAT NOT ONLY DID GOD MAKE YOU TO FOLLOW JESUS, BUT THAT JESUS IS TOTALLY WORTH FOLLOWING—FOR A LOT OF REASONS! JESUS IS WISE. JESUS IS POWERFUL. JESUS IS COMPASSIONATE. JESUS LOVES YOU. NEXT WEEK, YOU'LL LEARN A LITTLE BIT MORE ABOUT HOW YOU FOLLOW JESUS.

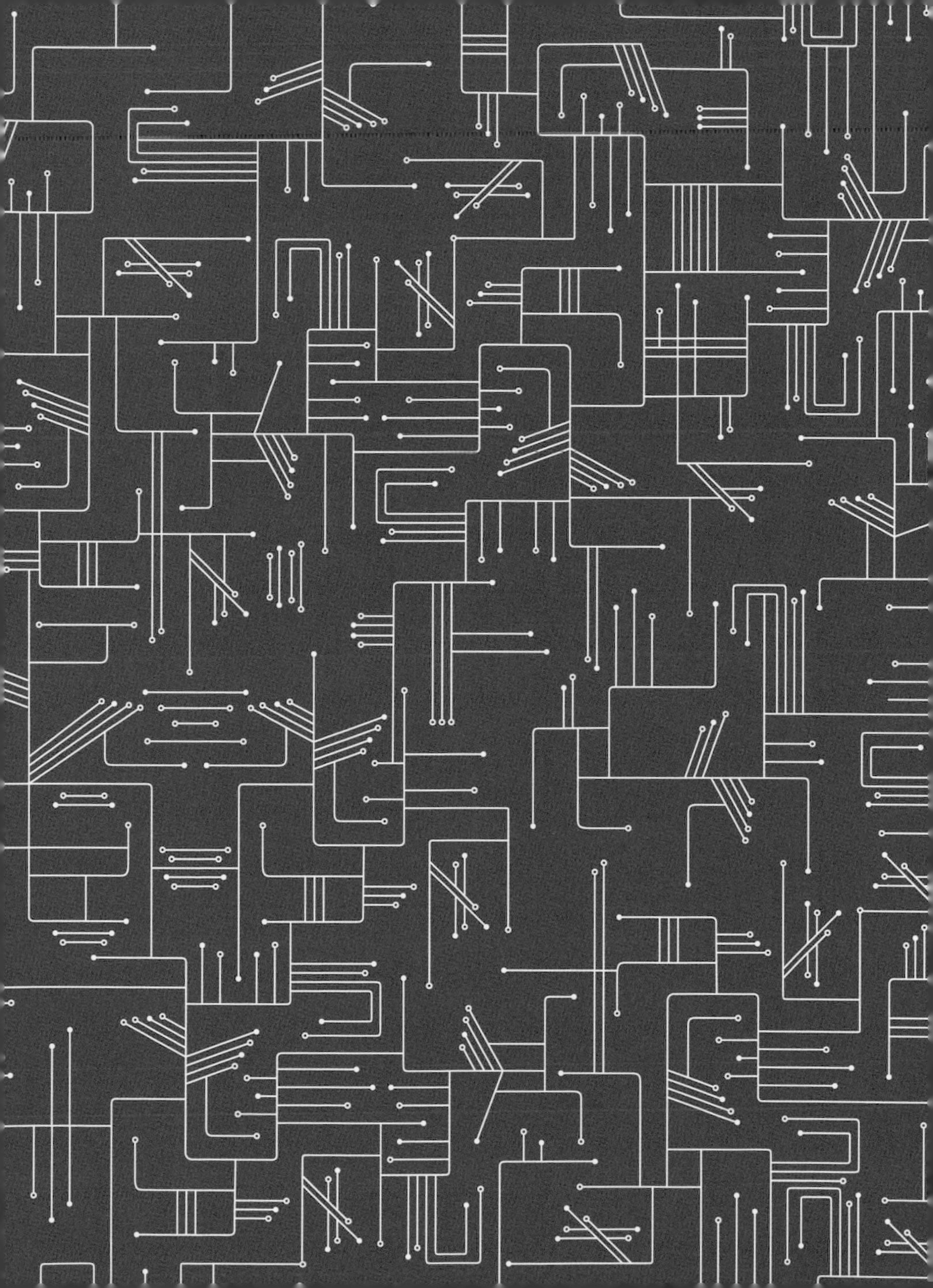

TRY THIS

Go somewhere.

God made you to follow Jesus. And usually when you follow someone, you have to go somewhere, right? So put on your best walking shoes. It's time to go somewhere.

Get permission before you just leave your home. You don't want anyone to be worried about you. Or ask a grown-up to go with you.

Where should you go? Well, that's up to you. But I'll give you some suggestions:

1. Go for a walk. Walk around your neighborhood. Or if you live in an apartment, walk around your apartment complex.
2. Go for a drive. Not you, of course. You're probably not old enough to drive. Find a grown-up to chauffeur you around. Go to a park or to a mall or to the zoo even.

While you're on this little journey, I want you to do some people watching. I know you've been told it's rude to stare at people. But just this once, it's okay. Look at people. Put yourself in their shoes for a moment. **Imagine what they're thinking.**

Notice how unique each person is. Who has different hair color than you? Skin color? Who's taller than you or shorter? Who looks like they could beat you in a race? Or a wrestling match?

As different as the people may be, they all have one thing in common. Jesus loves them. He loved them enough to die for them.

When you follow Jesus, it doesn't mean you have to go somewhere. But following Jesus does mean that you do your best to love the people He loves. Which means everyone.

WEEK EIGHT

DAY 36

God made you to love others.
(Acts 16:11-15a)

Someone once asked Jesus what the most important of all the commandments was. Jesus replied, "Love the Lord your God with all your heart and with all your soul. Love him with all your mind. And the second," He said, "is like the first. Love your neighbor as you love yourself."

Matthew 22:36

LOVE GOD
LOVE OTHERS

Then Jesus said, "Everything that is written in the Law and the Prophets is based on these two commandments." That means these two commandments are pretty important.

LOVE GOD
LOVE OTHERS

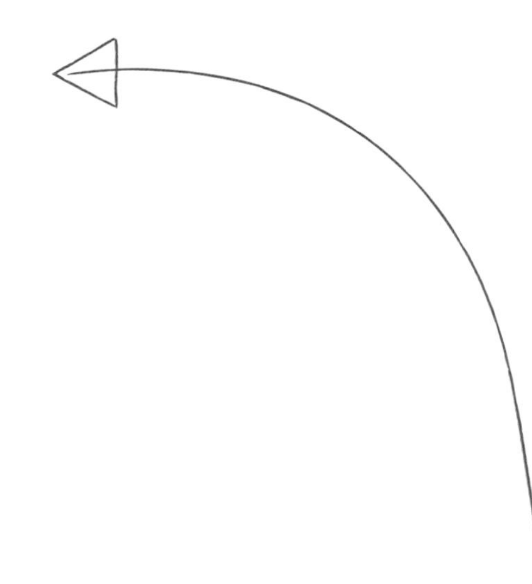

If you want to follow Jesus, these are the first two commandments you should focus on. Now because writing things down helps you remember, write those two commandments down here.

Good. There's a story in the Bible where the apostle Paul and his traveling companions demonstrate loving God and loving others. They were in the Roman colony of Philippi one Sabbath when they decided to walk down to the river to pray.

At the river, they discovered a group of women who had gathered together, so Paul and his companions began to speak with them.

They told the women the good news about Jesus, and one of them, a woman named Lydia, became a believer that day. She was baptized and then she invited them all over to her home.

It's not a really flashy story. There are no giants or slingshots or miracles, but it's a pretty great example of how to love. Paul and his friends could have gone down to the river, prayed, and gone home. They didn't have to talk to complete strangers about Jesus. And Lydia, too. She didn't have to listen and accept what they were saying. And she certainly didn't have to invite them all over to her home.

Love doesn't have to be really flashy. It doesn't have to be a grand gesture. Sometimes it is as simple as listening to someone. Or telling someone some good news. It's welcoming someone into your home. It's taking time out of your day for a stranger. Love is simple, but it can have a huge impact. **God made you to love others.**

Think of some ways that you can love others. Write a couple of them down. Remember, it can be simple.

....

....

....

....

....

....

....

....

....

....

IF IT WAS HARD FOR YOU TO THINK OF A FEW SIMPLE WAYS TO LOVE OTHERS, COME BACK TOMORROW. AND THE NEXT DAY. IN FACT, MAKE SURE YOU FINISH OUT THIS WEEK. YOU'RE GONNA *LOVE* IT.

DAY 37

Be kind to others.
(Ephesians 4:32a)

Have you ever heard of "random acts of kindness"? The idea is that you're kind to someone for no reason whatsoever. It's not their birthday or Christmas or Valentine's Day or Mother's Day. It's just a random day and you get them a gift or do something nice for them. I like the idea so much, this entire devotional day will be filled with random acts of kindness for you.

RANDOM ACT #1 You've earned a shoulder massage. Massage your own shoulders. Really dig in. You've had a long hard day and you deserve it.

One way you can love others is to **be kind to others.**

Ephesians 4:32 says —

Be kind
and tender to
one another.

RANDOM ACT #2 There's been enough thinking in this devotional. So for the next couple of minutes, think about whatever you want. It could be your favorite movie, what you're going to eat for breakfast tomorrow. You could think of a pineapple with legs walking on a tightrope over the Mississippi River. Good luck not thinking of that.

Being kind is actually pretty simple. Here, I'll give you a couple of kind things you can say to someone.

> ***"You look nice today, Mom."***
> ***"You're really good at drawing!"***
> ***"Is there anything I can do to help?"***
> ***"I can't believe how smart you are!"***

RANDOM ACT #3 Doodle time! Use the space below to draw whatever you want. You know? Doodle!

Kindness is more that what you say. It's what you do, too!

You can . . .

. . . pick someone flowers
. . . help out without being told
. . . make someone a card
. . . give someone a shoulder massage

RANDOM ACT #4 I wrote you a poem

Roses are red
Violets are blue
You're really neat
I have new socks

It's the thought that counts

Here's a challenge for you this week. Pick one person that you're going to be randomly kind to. It could be a parent, a brother or sister, a friend, or anyone you'd like. Don't tell them you picked them. Just be especially kind to them all week long. If you're an artist, make them something. Spend time with them doing something they like to do. Use words that will make them smile. It's all about them, so don't expect a reward for this. You're being kind, just because.

SOMETIMES BEING KIND TO PEOPLE ISN'T EASY. SO BE SURE TO ASK GOD TO HELP YOU FIND WAYS TO BE KIND EVEN TO PEOPLE WHO MAY NOT DESERVE IT.

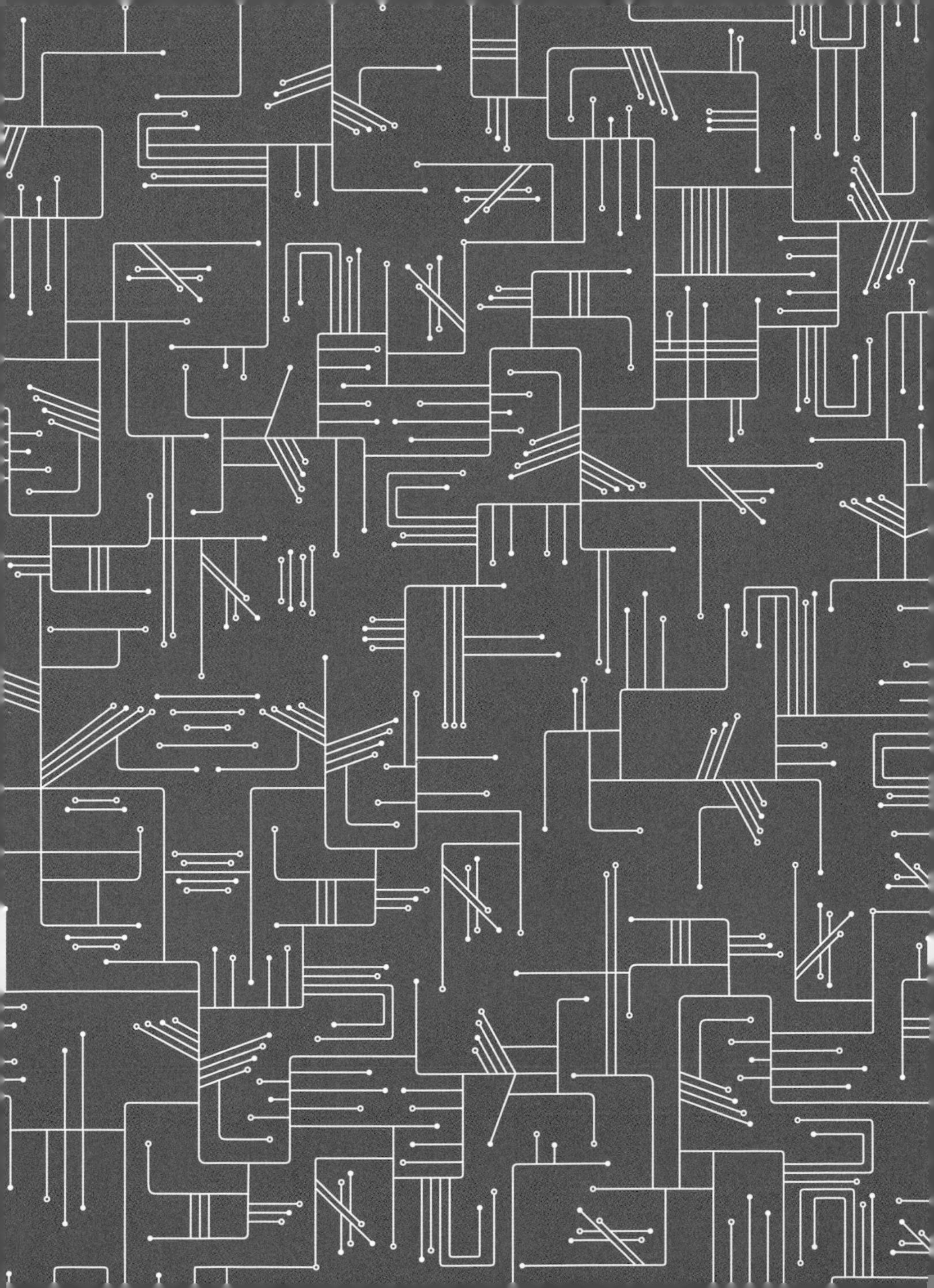

DAY 38

Be patient with others.
(Ephesians 4:2)

Count to ten. I'll wait.

Now count to twenty...

Count to thirty...

Now count to ten again...

Waiting is hard. Especially if you don't know what you're waiting for. Some people are good at waiting. We call them patient people. Some people are not so good. We call them impatient.

But it's important to learn patience. Because one of the ways you can love others is by **learning to be patient with others.**

Ephesians 4:2 says —

Don't be proud at all. Be completely gentle. Be patient. Put up with one another in love.

Here's a joke for you. Why was the doctor getting anxious? Because he had no patients! Get it? ... I didn't say it was a good joke.

QUICK TANGENT

Being patient with someone doesn't mean waiting with them. It means showing patience when someone makes you want to scream. Like . . .

THE TALKER This is that person who doesn't stop talking and won't let you get a word in, because everything they say is so important and they have to tell you every little detail about every little thing that happened in their day so you feel like you're trapped sometimes because you want to be polite and don't want to interrupt.

Try saying all this in one breath.

THE PRIMPER The person who has one last thing to do in the bathroom before you leave to go anywhere. Comb their hair, curl an eyelash, lip balm, etc... But you know that whatever it is they have to do, it will take at least a half hour.

THE KLUTZ This person can't help it that they're clumsy. But just in case, you'd better not let them go near anything that's valuable, because they're the ones who will certainly break it.

THE WINNER This person isn't doing anything wrong. In fact, it seems like they're always doing something right. This is the person who always gets cast as the lead in the school play. They get straight A's and they get picked first for every sports team. And they don't care who knows it.

Maybe you have a problem with one of these people. Maybe you are one of these people. So how can you be patient with someone who annoys you? How do you put up with one another in love?

There are a couple of things you can try. One is you can try putting yourself in the other person's shoes. Imagine what it's like to be them. **OR** close your eyes and count to ten when you start to feel annoyed. Sometimes all it takes is ten seconds to calm down and reset.

It's possible, though, that being patient is something you can't do on your own. That's where following Jesus comes in. When you believe in Jesus and follow Him, He sends His Spirit to help you. And sometimes, a lot of the time, you have to rely on God's Holy Spirit to help you do the things you can't do on your own.

SO NEXT TIME YOU FIND YOURSELF GETTING IMPATIENT WITH SOMEONE, A FRIEND OR A FAMILY MEMBER OR REALLY ANYONE, TAKE SOME TIME TO ASK GOD FOR HELP. ASK HIM TO GIVE YOU PATIENCE SO YOU CAN PUT UP WITH OTHERS IN LOVE.

DAY 39

Share with one another.
(Acts 2:44)

Find the second half of each of the words below.

1. SH _ _ _	PORT
2. COOPE _ _ _ _	EVE
3. BENE _ _ _	FIT
4. ENCOU _ _ _ _	PAIR
5. SUP _ _ _ _	ARE
6. RELI _ _ _	RAGE
7. IMP _ _ _ _	RATE
8. RE _ _ _ _	ROVE

If you've combined those words correctly, they should all spell ways we can love one another.

So far you've learned to be kind to others and to be patient with others. Today you're reading about what it means to **share with one another.** This is a tough one. Especially in a world where everything is mine, Mine, **MINE!!!** I earned it, so I should get to keep it **ALL** to myself!

But if you look at the way the believers in Jesus lived in the beginning, you might have a different perspective on things.

This may come as a shock to you, but we haven't always had churches the way we have them now. When the early church was just getting started, the believers met in people's homes. They ate together, prayed together, and worshipped together.

Acts 2:44 says —

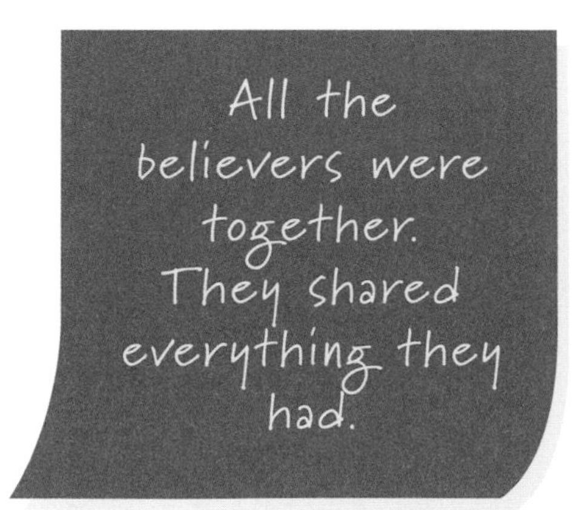

ANSWERS
1. share, 2. cooperate, 3. benefit,
4. encourage, 5. support, 6. relieve,
7.improve, 8. repair

They sold property and other things so they could give to people among them who were in need. And you know what? People noticed. The believers got along so well, people on the outside wondered, "What is it about these Jesus followers? I want to be like them." So more and more people became believers every day.

Wouldn't it be great if people today saw the way you were sharing with others and wanted to be more like you? If they said, "Wow! What is it about them? They're so kind and patient. And they share instead of keeping everything to themselves." If everyone who believed in Jesus chose to share with one another, people would notice in a big way.

Sharing starts in your own home. You share clothes and toys, TV time, computer time. You share a bathroom, maybe. What are some things you share around your home?

1. ....

2. ....

3. ....

4. ....

5. ....

6. ....

7. ....

8. ....

9. ....

10. ....

Like I said, sharing can be tough. Usually when you're sharing something, you're more concerned with what belongs to you or when it's your turn. It's time to change that. It's time to start putting the other person first every once in a while. God made you to love others, so you have it in you.

WHEN YOU HAVE TO SHARE SOMETHING AT HOME THIS WEEK, DON'T LOOK AT IT AS A BAD THING. SHARE WILLINGLY AND WITHOUT ARGUING. ASK GOD TO HELP YOU. REMEMBER, HE'S SENT YOU HIS HOLY SPIRIT WHEN YOU NEED HIM.

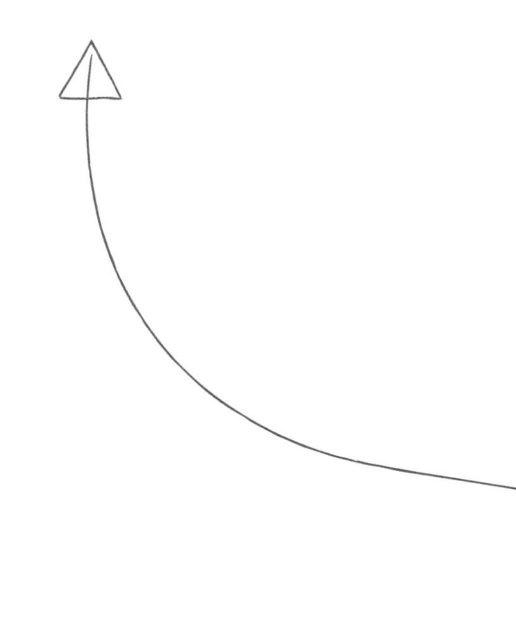

DAY 40

Stand up for others.
(Proverbs 31:8a)

How about a physical challenge? Try standing on one foot with this devotional balanced on your head. For an added challenge, close your eyes. Count how many seconds you can last. Go!

How long did you make it?

....

I made it for twenty seconds, which I think makes me pretty cool. If you beat my time, write **BOOYAH!** in the space below.

If you didn't beat my time, that's okay. You can practice later. Now I want to talk about what it means to stand up for someone.

We've talked about several ways you can love others. You can be kind to others, patient with others, and you can share with one another. And **you can stand up for others.**

QUICK TANGENT

You don't have to actually be standing to stand up for someone else. It's the one time you can stand up while sitting down.

I don't know if you've ever stood up for someone else, but it takes courage.

Or maybe you were like me and needed to be stood up for.

I was a small, shy kid in first grade when I started getting picked on by this boy named Michael. I should've asked the teacher for help, or my parents, but I was too shy. So every day at recess, Michael would shove me around and call me names. Until one day, another boy in my class, Chris, stood up for me. He told Michael not to mess with me anymore. Chris was bigger than Michael, so Michael left me alone after that.

We can't all be as lucky as I was. But I'll bet we'd have fewer people being picked on if we had more people standing up—if we had more people like Chris. I'm not saying you should be challenging the bully to a fight on the playground. I am saying if you see someone small or shy being treated in a way they shouldn't, speak up. Tell a teacher or a parent. Stand up for them.

Proverbs 31:8 says —

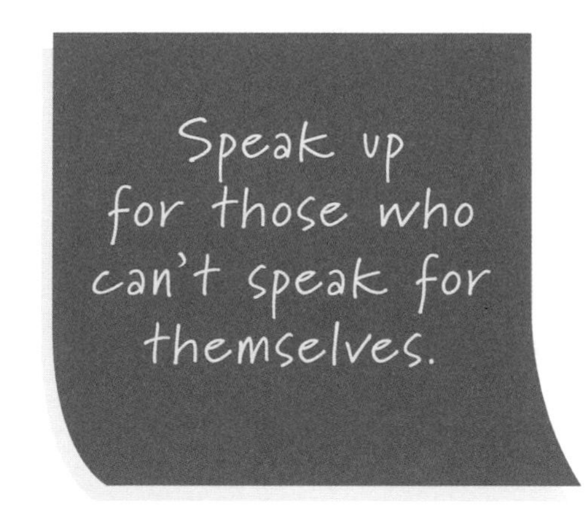

If you've ever had someone stand up for you, then you know how important it is to have someone like that. You could be that someone to someone else. You could be a voice for someone who's too shy to speak up. You could be their hero.

If you're being bullied or picked on, tell somebody, someone you trust.

If you see someone being bullied or picked on, do something, say something, be a hero.

If you pick on or bully others, stop it. It is not okay. And it's not too late for you to change.

STAND UP FOR OTHERS. THAT'S A WAY YOU CAN SHOW GOD'S LOVE. REMEMBER TO ASK GOD TO GIVE YOU THE COURAGE TO STAND UP AND SPEAK UP FOR THOSE WHO CAN'T SPEAK FOR THEMSELVES.

TRY THIS

Share something.

When asked what the greatest commandment was, Jesus said two things. Do you remember?

LOVE GOD
LOVE OTHERS

This week you read about how to love others, so I want you to invite a friend over and share something with them.

I'm not saying you have to share your favorite toy or video game. You can if you want, but what I'm talking about is sharing your time with someone. But here's the rule. You have to spend time doing something they want to do.

- **If they want to play video games, play video games.**
- **If they want to put on make-up, put on make-up.**
- **If they want to start a fire, you've picked the wrong friend.**
- **If you and your friend are stuck for ideas, here's a suggestion: Make a hoop glider.**

You can search online for "how to make a hoop glider" or you can follow these instructions.

What you need:

- **3x5 index card**
- **Tape**
- **Drinking straw**
- **Scissors**

1. Cut the index card into three equal strips 1 inch by 5 inches.

2. Make a loop with one of the strips and tape the ends together.

3. Make a larger loop using the two remaining strips, taping them end-to-end.

4. Tape the small loop to one end of the straw and tape the large loop to the other end as pictured.

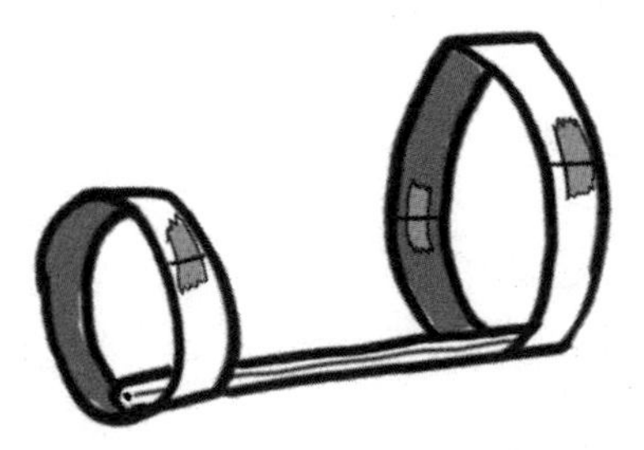

5. Hold the hoop glider by the straw with the hoops on top and throw!

When you're done, show your friend some love by letting them keep the hoop glider. You can always make another one later.

WEEK
NINE

DAY 41

God made you to do good.
(1 Corinthians 12:4-11)

Wow! You made it to the last week. Give me five!

Let's have one last recap. This time it's fill in the blank. The answers are at the bottom of this page, but I don't think you'll need them.

1. In the beginning, God made

   ....

2. God made a man named Adam and a woman named

   ....

3. They broke God's rule when they ate fruit from the tree of the knowledge of good and ....

4. When sin entered the world, people were

   .... from God.

5. God promised to send ....

   to help.

6. Jesus died on a cross to pay for our

   ....

7. God brought Jesus back from the

   ....

8. When you believe in Jesus, God sends His Holy

   .... to help you.

ANSWERS

1. everything, 2. Eve, 3. evil, 4. separated, 5. a Savior or Jesus, 6. sins, 7.dead, 8. Spirit

Now the question is, if God sends you His Holy Spirit to help, what does He help you do? Climb buildings? Shoot lasers with your eyes? Fly? Probably not.

1 Corinthians 12:7 says —

The Holy Spirit is given to each of us in a special way. That is for the good of all.

In other words, if you believe in Jesus, His Holy Spirit shows up in you in a unique way. Some of those ways are:

Wisdom	**Healing**	**Discernment**
Knowledge	**Miracles**	**Speak Languages**
Faith	**Prophesy**	**Interpret Languages**

These are kind of like super powers, but they're only used for one purpose—for doing good. **God made you to do good.**

This isn't the same as being good. It's not like, "Eat your peas like a good girl and you can get some ice cream."

It's doing good in the world. Doing something that really makes a difference. **Think for a minute. If you had all the money and resources in the world, what good would you do? Would you end hunger? End war? Save an animal from being endangered?**

....

....

....

....

....

....

....

Unfortunately, you don't have all the money in the world. ← *If you do, can we be friends?* So if you really want to do good in the world, you have to get creative. Or you have to have help. Which is where the Holy Spirit comes in. You'll have to rely on the Holy Spirit if you really want to do some good.

THIS WEEK, YOU'LL BE LEARNING ABOUT DIFFERENT WAYS YOU CAN DO GOOD. IT'S GOING TO TAKE A LITTLE BIT OF WORK ON YOUR PART, BUT I'M SURE YOU'RE UP TO IT.

DAY 42

**God made you to serve others.
(Philippians 2:4)**

DRAW THE EYES THAT WOULD MATCH THESE FACES.

The eyes really do make the face, don't they? Eyes are very important. And your eyes are important because they're the first stop on the way to doing something good.

Let me explain what I mean. God made you to do good, right? Well, before you can do anything good, first you have to see what good needs to be done. Once you see it, you can do it.

Philippians 2:4 says —

None of you should look out just for your own good. Each of you should also look out for the good of others.

LOOK OUT! That's what the Apostle Paul is telling you to do in that passage. **LOOK OUT!** There's good to be done somewhere.

What if we approached doing good like that? Like it was all-caps, urgent! **LOOK OUT!**

For instance, you're outside when your Dad pulls up with a car full of groceries. **LOOK OUT!** He might need some help. You rush up to the car in a flash!

"Can I assist you with those groceries, dear father?"

"Why, certainly, child. Whatever would I do without you?"

Or this... You're walking down the sidewalk when you see a friend from school crying. **LOOK OUT!** You hurry over to your friend!

"What seems to be the trouble, friend?"

"I've dropped my favorite action figure and now I can't find it!"

"Never fear! I will help you look for it!"

Now imagine if we lived in a world where everyone served each other in that way—if we all **LOOK OUT** for ways to help and serve others. It would be like living in a world full of superheroes.

A world full of superheroes would be pretty awesome! Or maybe there would be a lot of fights, because they'd all be trying to be the one who saved the day. But then, if they were all superheroes, would the day ever need saving? Something to ponder...

God made you to serve others. There is a lot of good to be done in the world. All you have to do is **LOOK OUT!**

Try something for me tomorrow. Really keep your eyes open for ways you can serve someone. It could be in your home or in your neighborhood or wherever you go. I'm going to make this easy on you. All you have to do (for now) is **LOOK.** You can serve those people if you want, but all I'm asking is that you practice seeing it for now. For your devotional tomorrow, I'm going to ask you what you saw, so keep track of it as best you can.

WHEN YOU PRAY NEXT, ASK GOD TO HELP YOU LOOK OUT FOR PEOPLE IN NEED. ASK HIM TO GIVE YOU OPPORTUNITIES TO SERVE THE PEOPLE AROUND YOU.

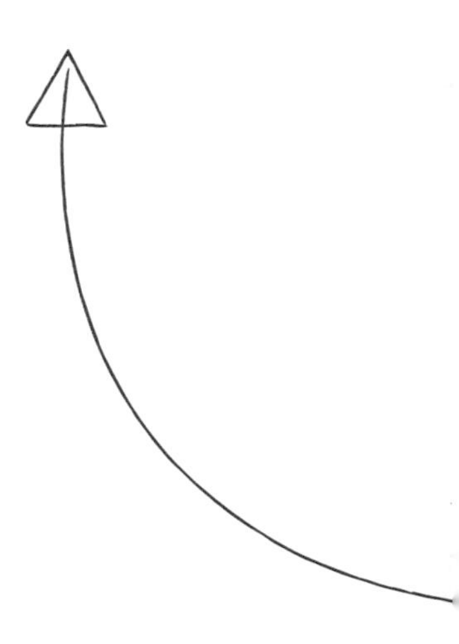

DAY 43

God made you to be generous.
(2 Corinthians 9:7)

Last time, I asked you to **LOOK OUT** for ways you could serve others and to keep track of what you saw.

WHAT DID YOU SEE?

....

....

If you didn't see anything, that's okay. But I don't want you to give up trying. Doing good takes practice, and it starts with what you see.

Another way you can do good is to be generous with what you have. **God made you to be generous.**

2 Corinthians 9:7 says —

Each of you should give what you have decided in your heart to give. You shouldn't give if you don't want to. You shouldn't give because you are forced to. God loves a cheerful giver.

God loves a cheerful giver. Here are some examples of a not so cheerful giver.

1. Fine! Take it! See if I care!
2. Okay, I'll give this to you, but you're gonna owe me big time.
3. *crying* Why did I give so much?
4. **HERE IS MY GIFT! I HOPE EVERYONE NOTICES!**

Those are some ways NOT to give. A cheerful giver gives in a different way.

1. A cheerful giver actually wants to give.
2. A cheerful giver doesn't expect anything in return.
3. A cheerful giver doesn't regret their gift.
4. A cheerful giver doesn't give for selfish reasons.

Are you a cheerful giver or a not so cheerful giver? Some of you may be thinking, "I'm not much of a giver at all, because I don't have much money."

Well, you're in luck. You don't have to be rich to be generous. In fact, you don't have to have any money at all. You can be generous if you have money, sure. But you can also be generous with your time, with your talent, and with your energy. Those are things you have without having to be filthy rich.

HOW CAN YOU BE GENEROUS WITH YOUR TIME?

....

....

....

....

You can spend time with someone who loves spending time with you even if you'd rather be doing something else.

HOW CAN YOU BE GENEROUS WITH YOUR TALENT?

....

....

....

....

You can paint a picture, sing a song, tell a joke, or do whatever it is you're talented at.

HOW CAN YOU BE GENEROUS WITH YOUR ENERGY?

....

....

....

....

You can help out around your home or wherever you see someone in need.

See? There are plenty of ways you can be a giver. The trick is being cheerful about it.

WHEN YOU PRAY, ASK GOD TO HELP YOU WITH YOUR ATTITUDE SO YOU CAN BE GLAD ABOUT BEING GENEROUS.

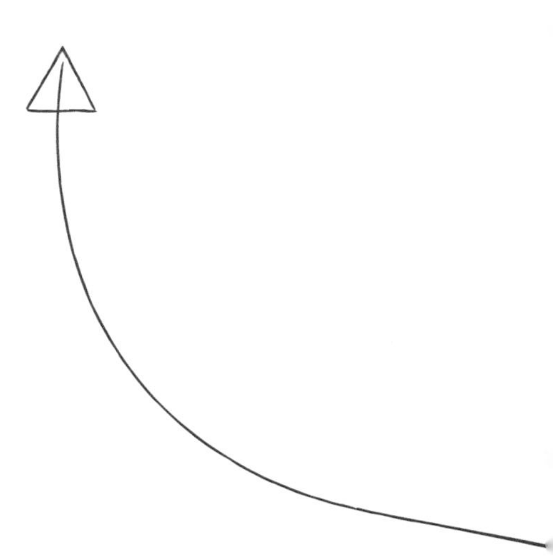

DAY 44

God made you to tell others about him. (Matthew 28:19-20)

Cue the spy movie music.

> Hello, Secret Agent Double O Positive, this is the Front Office. You're so close to the end now. Your secret mission, if you choose not to decline it, could be a dangerous one. Simply decode the following message using the formula A=1, B=2, C=3, D=4, etc... and follow the instructions therein. Should you fail to decipher the message, the answer will be given to you at the bottom of the next page. But don't give up too easily, Agent. Lives may depend on your success. Here is the message:

25•15•21
13•21•19•20
7•15
1•14•4
20•5•12•12

← Not really

This devotional will now self-destruct.

Okay, here's the truth. You're not really a spy. But you do have a mission. It's just not so secret. Jesus gave the disciples the same mission before He left the earth.

In Matthew 28:19 and 20, Jesus said —

"So you must go and make disciples of all nations. Baptize them in the name of the Father and of the Son and of the Holy Spirit. Teach them to obey everything I have commanded you."

I think Jesus is giving you and me the same mission. Go and make disciples. Teach them. Tell others about Jesus. Tell them about what He said and what He did. The wisdom, the miracles, how He died on a cross to pay for the sins of the world, and how He came back to life three days later.

This is good news that everyone needs to hear, and believe it or not, there are still people in the world who have never heard it. You don't have to worry about telling ALL the nations of the world all by yourself. You can start with your friends, or your neighbors, or people in your own family.

It may sound like an impossible mission, but Jesus also left the disciples with a promise. He said, "And you can be sure that I am always with you, to the very end."

The Holy Spirit will be with you to help you on your mission.

YOU MUST GO AND TELL

ANSWERS

When you tell someone about Jesus, you don't have to have all the answers. You don't have to know the Bible backwards and forwards. You just talk about what you know and if someone asks you a question that you don't know the answer to, you can say three words. "I don't know." You're never going to know everything. That's part of what having faith is all about: believing without knowing everything.

IS THERE SOMEBODY YOU KNOW WHO DOESN'T KNOW THE STORY OF JESUS?

YES NO

Think about their name or names. Write them down if you feel comfortable.

....

....

....

....

IF YOU THOUGHT OF SOMEONE, TAKE A MOMENT TO PRAY FOR THAT PERSON OR PEOPLE. ASK GOD TO PREPARE THEIR HEARTS FOR THE STORY OF JESUS. ASK HIM TO HELP YOU FIND A GOOD MOMENT TO TELL THEM WHAT YOU KNOW ABOUT JESUS.

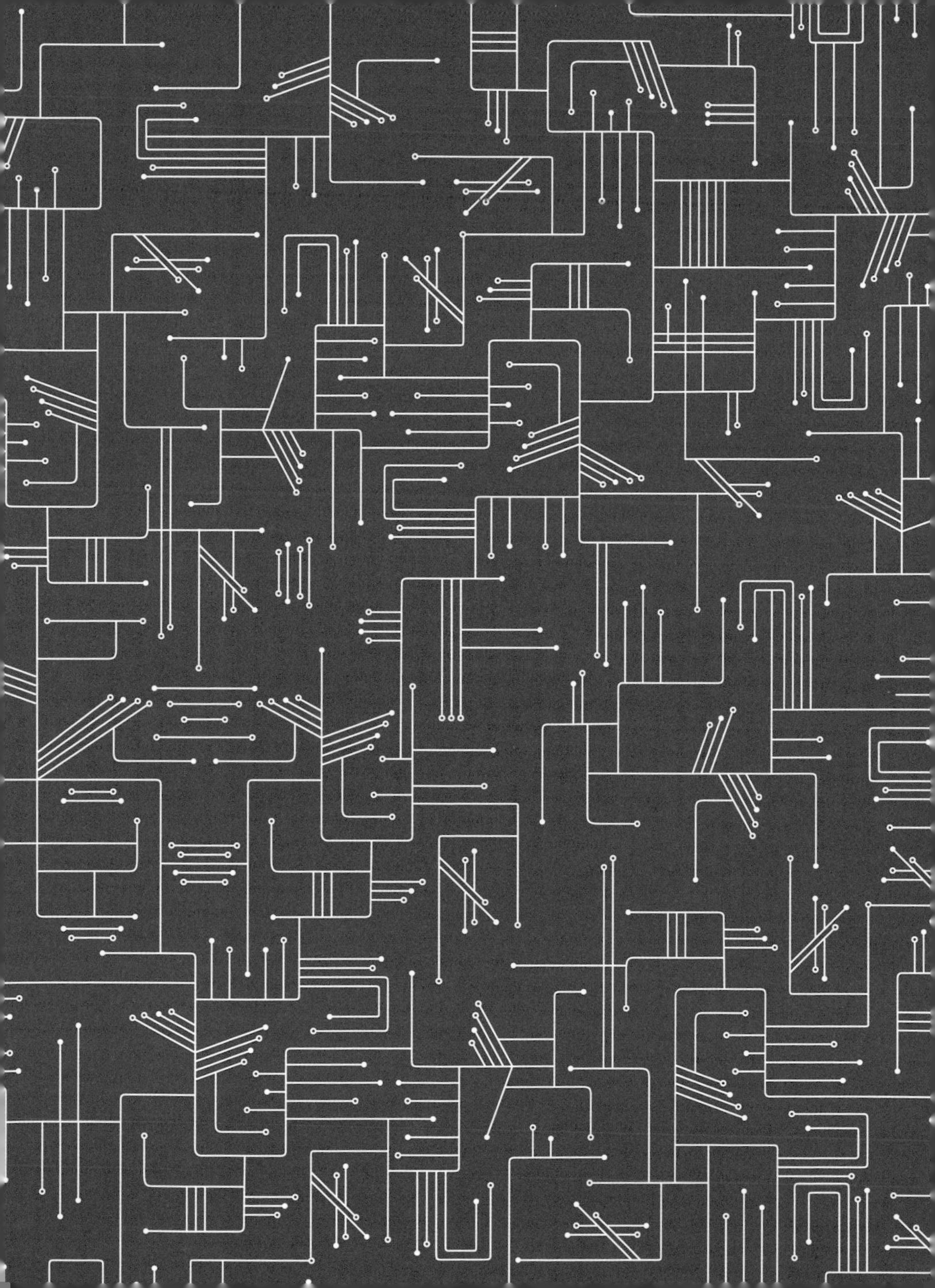

DAY 45

You were made to shine your light. (Matthew 5:14-16)

I don't know if you can remember nine weeks ago, but this devotional started out a little dark. A lot dark actually. It started at the very beginning when there was nothing. Until . . . God said, "Let there be light." And there was light!

The rest of God's big story—the Bible—has lots of dark moments –

...Adam and Eve eating fruit from the wrong tree
...Joseph being sold into slavery
...Jesus dying on a cross

And the Bible has a lot of light, too.

...David defeating Goliath
...Joseph becoming second in command of Egypt
...Jesus rising from the dead

And you'll find that the world today has some darkness, too.

...Sickness
...Divorce
...Bullies
...Broken bones
...Sin

The world needs light. Where will it come from?

YOU. The answer is you.

Matthew 5:14

Jesus said, "You are the light of the world." Jesus was talking to a huge crowd of people who were following Him, and I think He was also talking to you and me. You are the light that can shine in a dark world. So don't keep it hidden. You wouldn't hide a lamp under a bowl. The lamp would serve no purpose. No, if you have a light, you let it shine.

So how do you let your light shine?

Jesus goes on to say in Matthew 5:16 —

"In the same way, let your light shine so others can see it. Then they will see the good things you do. And they will bring glory to your Father who is in heaven."

You can let your light shine by doing good.

You do good by following Jesus.

When you follow Jesus, you love God and you love others.

And when you love God and love others, people will notice and God will get the glory for it!

And that's really what it's all about. Shining the light of Jesus so the Creator of Everything can get the glory.

So shine your light.

Do good.

Follow Jesus.

Love God. Love others.

Be the you God made you to be.

READ THE DEVOTIONAL AGAIN IF YOU CAN'T REMEMBER HOW TO DO THOSE THINGS. BUT I THINK YOU CAN. YOU'RE REALLY SMART.